Best Wish
Douglas L

Lest We Forget

VOLUME ONE

by

DOUGLAS LAMB

The photographs
are by
Douglas Lamb & Stephen J. Reaney

And Then there was one

Pictured below are the preserved remains of the last of the many hundreds of cementation furnaces which for so many years produced the huge amounts of raw steel which made Sheffield a great industrial city. It is sited in Doncaster Street, off Shalesmoor. This street was named after Daniel Doncaster's steel company which used to be situated there. The furnace was restored with the help of the Midland Bank plc.

The large square plaque attached to the railings in front of this now silent and unique museum piece tells all there is to know about the process. Here is part of the inscription:-

"This steel making furnace is the only example of its type to survive intact in Britain. It was one of several operating on this site for almost 100 years by Daniel Doncaster & Sons and its last use in 1951 brought to a close the oldest steel making technology.

The process by which steel was made in this furnace was known as the cementation process, first developed in Germany around 1600 and introduced into Britain a few years later. It was not adopted in Sheffield until 1709, but from that time onwards, until the advent of newer technology in the late 19th century, it played a key role in the development of the Sheffield steel industry and these large conical furnaces became a characteristic feature of the city's industrial architecture....."

THE FIRST HOLOCAUST

He was right, you know
the man who wrote - they will not care.
The grandchildren will not care.
I've been; I've seen and touched the moss,
and grass and broken stone
which marks the places
where the young men lie
and read the words which tell
of sons yet missing still or lost.
It doesn't matter now, not any more.
Those who wept for them and
shared their pain and were there then,
have gone to seek the truth and
find that the fight was never won...

Douglas Lamb
(b 1941)

This isn't a guide book, neither is it a history book, it was never intended to be either of these. Rather, it is a random collection of objects of interest which it might be worthwhile for a person to go out of their way to see, and all within the boundaries of the City of Sheffield.

These things, both the obvious and the obscure, which disprove the words that I have so often heard spoken, "There's nowt much here, in Sheffield!"

There is, you know. More than even I thought possible!

Who is this bloke?

ISBN 0 9534267 0 X

First published in 1998 by Pickards Publishing

Published and Printed by Pickards Publishing

Unit 11 • Riverside Park • Sheaf Gardens • Sheffield S2 4BB

Telephone 0114 2757222 or 2757444

Lest We Forget

Introduction to Volume One

"The persons I pity, who know not the city."
William Jeffery Prowse 1836 - 1870

SHEFFIELD isn't and never has been a city of great statues. In the past there have been a few; those great monuments to dead monarchs and past wars, but during the last decades the city has altered almost beyond recognition and even this meagre collection has mostly disappeared from sight, shunted into retirement to decay slowly away from the public eye. Out of sight and, to a large extent, out of mind.

Today in the centre of Sheffield, the only statue in the old mould - large, bronze, covered in bird droppings and commemorating a king - is in Fitzalan Square. It is dedicated to King Edward VII, known as The Peacemaker, at least to some, but since the little used square was cleaned up and planted with trees, even his bulk is slowly disappearing from sight.

There are, however, plenty of memorials to be found in the city and also in the surrounding urban area and villages. Some of these are little more than a discreet and ignored plaque on a wall; others are hidden in churches or other buildings. Still more are merely graves. But they are there, they just need looking for.

When Sheffield grew in size to be one of the main cogs in Britain's huge global empire and the place sprouted from being a small town with a river into a large and smoke-logged, heavy industrial giant, it produced along the way many great men. Citizens who invented things, developed ideas, became painters or sculptors, poets, writers and actors. Others who created huge industrial and engineering empires with names still known today or who built structures still existing now. To many of these formidable men there are small and neglected memorials; to some there are none!

In this book, which is the first of a proposed series, I have scoured the area in an attempt to produce a record of what there actually is still to be seen. This is decreasing as the years slide by and as the modern world ceases to produce the type of person or event which merits a reminder and stops looking back to the past upon which today's reality is built.

Soon perhaps even the war memorials will go, overtaken by events and indifference, but at least Sheffield's own local highwayman will probably still have a memorial plaque!

The most densely populated areas of memorabilia are without a doubt the graveyards, cemeteries, burial grounds, call them what you will, and naturally many mentions of graves and tombs will occur throughout this book.

As I have already written, this isn't intended to be a history book, there are plenty of those already; also, it isn't my aim that the resting places of the worthies who have coloured and seasoned Sheffield's past should be a major part of its contents. There will be well known names mentioned, but in the main the names written here will belong to ordinary people. Ordinary, except that for some reason they have just that little twist to their memorials - a small thing that lifts them above the average; simple probably, but interesting quirks that set their gravestone apart from the other hundreds of honestly bland graves which stud the grass of the city's burial grounds.

The two brothers, for example, who died years apart and on other sides of the world, but who were both 22 years old when they died; or the man who served as chaplain to Admiral Lord Nelson on his flagship, HMS Victory, at the Battle of Trafalgar. That sort of difference.

Killed on the first day of the Battle of the Somme.

Every graveyard or cemetery has its mixture of graves. It became, with some classes of citizens, fashionable to be buried in a certain place. Ecclesall churchyard, for example, is well stocked with wealthy cutlery manufacturers and merchants, but there are also several graves or memorials commemorating men who died on 1st July, 1916, the first day of the Battle of the Somme. In Tinsley Park Cemetery, a former town councillor has a large obelisk; but the boy of 19 years, who died while attempting to save his friend from drowning in the Attercliffe Canal, also has a memorial provided by public subscription.

Here in Sheffield, several of the older cemeteries have sections crowded with large, expensive and overly ornate tombs - monuments to the eminent Victorians who made their mark, in one way or another, on the city - grand funerary edifices which were as much an attempt at immortality as to impress their surviving contemporaries. Here, visibly and tangibly, is the tragedy of temporal human existence and it lends to these cemeteries, Walkley, The General Cemetery, Tinsley Park, Ecclesall and others, a grand yet mournful ambience. Many of these tombstones pay small homage to Christianity and some of the architects have been allowed free rein to indulge their own lofty ideas. They remain stone curiosities, commemorating worthy citizens who today are largely forgotten.

After so many visits to so many graveyards and cemeteries, I am left with one question which I find hard to answer. How long are people remembered? If they are well known, by both the general public and also their families; if not, then just by their families? The answer, if there is one, must be that there isn't a great deal of difference between the two groups. If anything, the slight edge in longevity of remembrance is in favour of the ordinary person. This is, of course, only in my experience, but as I have quite a few "graveyard hours" under my belt, it may carry some weight.

I have seen the graves of some of the greatest men who have ever lived in Sheffield; men who were legends, who built great steel and cutlery empires and who employed huge swathes of the local workforce. Men whose desire to succeed and whose specialised knowledge helped to build the British Empire.

Most of these men died in the latter end of the 19th century or perhaps a little later, or earlier, and almost without exception their last resting places are, if not badly neglected, then at best merely surviving intact. There are several examples that I can give. William Butcher (c1791-1870). This man, along with his brother, Samuel, formed Butcher Brothers, which was one of the largest cutlery manufacturers in the world for a large part of the 19th century, and yet his grave in Ecclesall churchyard is so covered with ivy that it is difficult to locate; that of his brother, whose tomb is nearby, was also hard to find. Samuel Osborn (1826-1891), a pioneer toolsteel maker of huge importance to the world of engineering, has a family tomb at the side of the church in Ecclesall churchyard, but I asked the sexton where it was and when he didn't know, I only chanced upon it by luck.

These two men have only been dead just over 100 years, and yet while their names may grace the pages of history books, no-one bothers, not even their families, to make any effort to preserve their graves.

There is a large building company, Henry Boot & Sons, who are still very much to the forefront in the business. They didn't even know in which graveyard their founder, his wife and daughters, were buried until I told them, and he only died in 1931!

On the other side of the coin, I have found beautifully kept graves, humble in the extreme, in several churchyards and have on several occasions watched as flowers were placed and the grave surround tidied. In these cases the graves have dated from, at the latest, the First World War.

I wonder if this "out of sight, out of mind" attitude is common only to Sheffield or whether it is usual throughout the whole of the country? Either way, I find it very difficult to understand. In years past, family graves were cherished as part of the family circle.

I have photographed many graves which are very old and the expense which must have been incurred in the purchase of these beautifully carved slabs of stone or slate would have been immense to a normal working family. Perhaps that is why they were so well looked after. It would, however, be far kinder to think that it was through affection.

Today in Sheffield, and this is probably true nationwide, as the 20th century closes and cremation becomes more popular as the way of ending a funeral, even the few new memorial stones are small, plain and sober in style. The reasons for this are several. The sheer expense of a funeral is daunting enough, without the added cost of a fancy memorial. Family groups are smaller now and less close-knit in their lives. Even, perhaps, the insistence of members of the clergy or the council which owns the ground, that inscriptions cover only the barest of details. No flowery phrases or verses here.

What we have left, as far as burial grounds are concerned, are all we are likely to get. There won't be many new ones opened, only old ones closed or gradually left to moulder away.

It is a shame, of course, but these areas of land are dead ground in more senses than one. Many, if not most of them, are unkempt at best and completely derelict and reverting to nature at worst. Some are never visited by relatives at all and are only explored by persons like me, blackberry hunters, dog walkers or joggers. Graveyards have always been places for peaceful thought and reflection, quiet sanctuaries, and still are, but as far as today's builders and developers are concerned, they are merely unused wasteground. Once, a consecrated plot in a churchyard was hallowed ground for centuries, but no more. Memories are very short and businessmen have long purses. Very little, especially when money is an issue, is sacred.

Except for a few elderly people, no-one remembers St Paul's Church which stood where the Peace Gardens used to be. It was a large, imposing and important building surrounded by its own graveyard in which were buried, among others, the remains of Thomas Boulsover, the discoverer of the process by which Sheffield Plate was produced. Then, due to an even then short sighted council, it disappeared and, when plans for the area failed to materialise, the site was turned into a haven for drunks and drop-outs. Recently, new developments for the area have begun.

That was in the 1930's. In the 1990's, no-one thought twice about what to do when more space was needed to allow Supertram to run down Church Street. It was simple to dig up a large portion of the cathedral graveyard and remove the remains of the bodies which had lain there in peace for many years. They were getting in the way of the excavator. How long will it be before the cemetery which overlooks Rivelin Valley, that bird crammed and peaceful wilderness, is under tarmac and concrete?

The bold and slightly arrogant solid granite tombstones which have brooded for so many years in Sheffield's cemeteries and graveyards are the

Endcliffe Park

last that will be planted. The complicated inscriptions, little histories in themselves, will blur and fade as the natural aging processes of wind, rain and frost do their work. Most of the members of families who were once proud to visit the plots are themselves now dead and their descendants are busy living their own lives and have no interest in wasting time on a long dead ancestor they never knew.

Even now, churchyards which surround popular churches have the gravestones removed, laid down to make paths or rooted up and propped against the walls. It makes it easier to cut the grass. No-one is interested in the few feet of earth beneath and tombstones get in the way. Don't give the vicar a hard life, he will probably be too busy worrying about his empty church to be bothered with the fate of dead parishioners!

When all the burial grounds have gone, we will know that we have been improved once again by progress and most of us will accept it without thinking twice, or accept it as an accomplished fact. Most of us will!

In order to include as many monuments as possible in the space available, I have taken the liberty, where necessary, of truncating some of the inscriptions to leave only the interesting parts.

If I had included, in this one book, all the interesting information that I have already collected, the result would have been a huge, fat and expensive tome, priced by necessity out of the range of the very people who I am trying to attract.

Because of this, I will be following up this first folio with a series of several others. These I hope to produce at regular intervals of not more than a year. All being well, eventually everything of interest will be included in one or other of the books.

Books Consulted

Sheffield between 1835 and 1935, Folios 2 & 4 *by David Robins*

Old Sheffield Town *by J Edward Vickers*

Popular History of Sheffield *by J Edward Vickers*

The Odd, Amusing and Unusual in Sheffield *by J Edward Vickers*

Giants of Sheffield Steel *by Geoffrey Tweedale*

The English Civil War in South Yorkshire & North Derbyshire *by Vernon Thornes*

Sheffield Industrial Museum, Kelham Island *by Peter G Smithurst*

Sheffield - History & Guide *by David Fine*

Kelham Island - A Visitor's Guide *by Peter Smithurst & Nicola Moyle*

Yorkshire Greats - Great Achievers From Yorkshire's Past *by Dawn G. Robinson - Walsh*

Creators Of The Age Of Steel (Collection)

Hallamshire Worthies. Historic Personages of Sheffield *by W. Odom*

Civic Art In Sheffield *by E.D. Mackerness & others*

Steel City *by Geoffrey Tweedale*

Pioneers For A Century. The story of Osborn Steels

Sheffield, Its Story & Its Achievements *by Mary Walton*

Sheffield At The Front (Boer War Pictorial Survey, 1899 - 1901)

The Picture of Sheffield (1824 Collection)

Reminiscences of Old Sheffield *by R E Leader*

The Story of Sheffield *by John Derry*

Old Churchyards of Sheffield *by William J J Glassby*

The Making of Sheffield *by J H Stainton 1865 - 1914*

Illustrated Guide to Sheffield *by Pawson & Brailsford*

The Village of Ecclesfield *by David Hey*

An Old Sheffield Diary 1775-1845 *by Septimus Lister*

The Sheffield Knife Book *by Geoffrey Tweedale*

The History of the City of Sheffield. (Volumes I - III) 1843 - 1993. Sheffield Academic Press

A Complete History of the Great Flood of Sheffield *by Samuel Harrison*

Crookes: The History of a Sheffield Village, 1982 *by Crookes Local History Group*

Crookes Revisited *by Crookes Local History Group*

Pedigree of the Jeffcock Family (1932) *by W P Jeffcock*

Parkin Jeffcock, Civil and Mining Engineer (Profile)

Jeffcock, Parkin (Newspaper cuttings relating to Sheffield, Vol. 37)

The Flowing Stream - The Jeffcock Family of Handsworth, Vol 5, No. 3, Winter 1984 (collection of writings)

History of the Sheffield Battalion *by Richard A Sparling*

A Pub On Every Corner *by Douglas Lamb*

Sheffield Curiosities *by Duncan and Trevor Smith*

Life and Times at Bracken Hill *by Beryl Greaves*

Grenoside Heroes 1914 - 1918 *edited Margaret Batson*

The Lord's House: A History of Sheffield's Roman Catholic Buildings 1570 - 1990 *by Denis Evinson*

The Story of St Philip's Church, Sheffield: A Centenary Record, 1828 - 1928 *by Canon W. Odom*

150 Years of Architectural Drawings - Hadfield, Cawkwell & Davidson, Sheffield,1834 - 1984

Chantrey Land *by Harold Armitage*

Sheffield 200 Years Ago *by Joseph Woolhouse*

The Sheffield Iron & Steel Works, Brown, Bayley & Dixon, 1871 - 1971

Sheffield Obituary compiled *by Peter Harvey*

The House of Cockayne (house publication)

Quality of Sheffield (magazine collection, 1957, vol. 4)

A quotation from a letter received from the Imperial War Museum

A copy of the regimental history of Lt. G. Lambert VC -
The York & Lancaster Regimental Museum, Rotherham

Papers collected by Mr Loosemore regarding the career of his father, Sgt. A Loosemore VC, DCM.

Again, as in my previous book, "A Pub On Every Corner", I must extend to all the dedicated staff of the Local Studies Library, Sheffield City Library, my thanks for the help they gave me.

Also my thanks to Stephen J. Reaney for his invaluable technical work on the photographs

Not forgetting Diane Gascoyne,
a mine of information, a loyal supporter and a great help.

CONTENTS

FRONTISPIECE

THE CRIMEAN WAR MEMORIAL

"For what can war but endless war still breed?"

John Milton 1608 - 1674

THIS memorial, one of the largest and most impressive in Sheffield, is dedicated to the men of the city who sacrificed their lives in the Crimean War against Russia which lasted through 1854 - 1855. Although an exact figure is not known, it is believed that about 100 men from this area died in this needless little war. It was erected in 1863 originally in the area now known as Moorhead.

In the competition held to select the designer of the memorial, the scheme proposed by George Goldie of the local firm of architects, Hadfield & Goldie (now practicing as Hadfield, Cawkwell, Davidson & Partners) was placed second. However, the promotors of the competition preferred his design and a revised version of this was built.

The base of the monument is made of Darley Dale stone with originally a 58 foot high column of Aberdeen granite topped by a capital and supporting a seated figure of Queen Victoria representing "Honour". She used to be depicted holding a sheathed sword in one hand and a laurel wreath in the other, but this part of the statue is damaged and both the hand and the wreath appear to be missing.

When it was first erected, there were two cannons, one either side of the main plinth, but these have since disappeared. The figure of the queen was designed by Henry Lane.

In 1957, to allow for road and building development works to take place, it was dismantled and removed to its present obscure site in the Botanical Gardens where it was re-assembled, but minus the column which has since been put to use in a school playground in Hammond Street, broken down into its individual segments and used as climbing blocks. This just about sums up Sheffield City Council's off-hand attitude towards what should be the treasures of the city!

Two streets at least that I know of were named to commemorate the Crimean War - Alma Street and Balaclava Road, there may have been others. This practice was continued with later conflicts - Omdurman Street after Lord Kitchener's victory in the Sudan in 1898 which also saw the last full scale cavalry charge launched by the British Army, an event which numbered Winston Churchill among its participants; and Ladysmith Avenue taken from the Boer War at the turn of the 19th century are two examples.

I haven't been able to find any streets named after First World War battles, but then, there wasn't really very much to celebrate, was there?

The monument is inscribed:-

THIS MONUMENT IN
MEMORY OF THOSE
NATIVES OF SHEFFIELD
WHO FELL IN THE WAR
IN THE CRIMEA
WAS ERECTED BY PUBLIC
SUBSCRIPTIONS 1863

CHAPTER ONE

POETRY AND POLITICS

"Learn'd or unlearn'd, we are all politicians."

Soame Jenyns 1704 - 1787

"Poetry is the spontaneous overflow of powerful feelings"

William Wordsworth 1770-1850

THE three men who make up the first part of this chapter were none of them Sheffield born, but all of them either spent the most important period of their lives in the city or achieved here the actions by which they are remembered. Two have large and expensive statues commemorating their lives and one has only a rather lopsided tombstone in an unkempt section of a graveyard. Such is life, and death!

To some it would seem only natural to begin this series of books with a traditional statue and also that it should be of one of the two " royal " images that Sheffield owns, Queen Victoria and King Edward VII. I can't think why. I'm starting off with a Yorkshireman!

EBENEZER ELLIOTT

Ebenezer Elliott, the man's very name merits first place, was born in Masbrough, near Rotherham, on 17th March, 1781. All his adult life he was absorbed by both poetry and politics and quite often these twin interests merged.

He became a very active radical politician much involved in the working mans' fight against the electorial system. But his most famous campaign, and the one which formed the subject of some of his most famous poems, was for the reform of the Corn Laws. It was because of these particular poems that he earned his enduring nickname, "The Corn Law Rhymer".

His father was in the iron business and when he was 16 years old, following a basic education, Elliott joined him. The company unfortunately failed and Elliott, by then married and with a dependant family, was left virtually destitute. However, when he was nearing 40 years old, he managed to borrow sufficient capital to set up in business for himself and to this end moved with his wife and family and settled in Sheffield. He proved that on his own he could succeed and by the time he was 60 years old, had done sufficiently well to be able to retire, leave the smoky hell of industrial Sheffield and move to Great Houghton. There he spent the remaining years until his death, pottering with poetry and other literary works.

When Elliott died, on 1st December, 1849, he was buried in Darfield churchyard where his grave, to the south of the church, can still be seen.

Ebenezer Elliott was an extremely popular man with the working class of the surrounding area who recognised, no doubt, that all his life he had had their interests at heart. A collection was taken up and £600 was raised to commission a statue in his memory. It was designed by NN Burnard (1818-1878) and erected in Sheffield Market Place in 1854. It was later moved, to facilitate road widening, of course, in 1875, to its present position in Weston Park.

Elliott's most famous poems, "The Village Patriach" , "The Ranter" and "The Splendid Village" are known as the Corn Law Rhymes and were written at a time when these laws, which resulted in the maintenance of an artificially high price for bread, in all but name a Tax on Bread, the workmans' staple diet, were causing much civil disorder in the country.

His work has inevitably been compared to that other Sheffield poet, James Montgomery, and many people who have read both, feel that when Elliott was in full flow and writing about a subject dear to his heart, his work is generally superior. The poems that he produced during those periods of inspiration can be rightly classed as true literature - writing that will not be forgotten - and that is a rare thing.

Ebenezer Elliott in Weston Park

JAMES MONTGOMERY

The eldest son of missionary parents, James Montgomery was born in November, 1771 at Irvine, Ayrshire. His parents wanted him to follow them into the ministry and to that end he was sent to study at the Morovian School at Fulneck, Leeds, but following the death of his parents' in the West Indies, the school decided that he had no vocation for the church, or possibly the financial position had altered with his parents' death, and he was sent to work in business.

Montgomery already had a deep interest in poetry and he did in fact travel to London in search of a publisher for some of his work. This excursion was a failure and he spent the following few years employed by a grocer in Wath upon Dearne.

In 1792, he obtained a position as a clerk in the Hartshead offices of the local Sheffield newspaper, The Sheffield Register, where he was far more at home. In 1794, the editor of the newspaper, James Gales, became embroiled in the politics of the day, especially those concerning the French Revolution, which was raging at the time. Mr Gales had very decided views on the subject which were directly opposite to those held at the time by the British Government and he was forced to flee to America to save his skin, leaving the editorship of the newspaper in the hands of the young James Montgomery.

This was just the opportunity that Montgomery was waiting for and he seized it eagerly. He was soon firmly ensconced as editor and he re-named the paper, The Iris. For the first few years of his editorship he found that his own radical political views were unpopular with the Government and he was in fact twice jailed at York Castle for seditious libel, in the first instance for publishing a ballad about the French revolutionist capture of the Bastille. For this he was jailed for three months and fined £20. The second clash with the authorities cost him his liberty for six months and £30 in fines. This second punishment was for printing an article about a riot which broke out in Sheffield, in the Norfolk Street area. During the fracas, the Army Volunteers were ordered to fire on the crowd and this panic induced action resulted in the deaths of two men and the wounding of others. It was Montgomery's criticism of the young officer who gave the order to fire which was sufficient to land him again in prison.

However, from about 1796, the newspaper became popular and Montgomery, as its editor, was accepted into Sheffield "society" and became one of its most respected members. Although he retired from the control of The Iris in 1825, he continued to take an active part in the affairs of the town until his death on April 30, 1854.

He received a public funeral and his body was buried with great ceremony in the General Cemetery, Ecclesall Road. A bronze statue listing his achievements and some of his poetry was erected over his grave. It was designed by John Bell (1811-1895) and cast by the Coalbrookedale Iron Company about 1860. It was removed in 1971, refurbished, and repositioned in the graveyard beside Sheffield Cathedral where it may be admired today.

Part of the inscription on the base of his statue reads:-

Front face:-

MONTGOMERY
JAMES MONTGOMERY
BORN IRVINE, SCOTLAND NOVEMBER 4th 1771
DIED AT THE MOUNT, SHEFFIELD
(AFTER A RESIDENCE IN THE TOWN OF 62 YEARS)
APRIL 30th 1854.
IN THE 83rd YEAR OF HIS AGE.
THE TEACHERS, SCHOLARS AND FRIENDS
OF SUNDAY SCHOOLS IN SHEFFIELD
ASSISTED BY PUBLIC SUBSCRIPTION
HAVE ERECTED THIS MONUMENT
IN MEMORY OF THEIR REVERED TOWNSMAN
MDCCCLXI

Rear face:-

HERE LIES INTERRED
BELOVED BY ALL WHO KNEW HIM
THE CHRISTIAN POET
PATRIOT
AND PHILANTHROPIST.
WHERE EVER POETRY IS READ
OR CHRISTIAN HYMNS ARE SUNG
IN THE ENGLISH LANGUAGE
!! HE BEING DEAD YET SPEAKETH !!
BY THE GENIUS PIETY AND TASTE
EMBODIED IN HIS WRITINGS.

Montgomery wrote several hundred poems and hymns during his long life, but these are mostly forgotten today. Although he has a reputation as Sheffield's best known poet and man of letters, he was, I consider, in fact nothing really special. The main reason, I feel, for the popularity of his work was that, as the editor of one of the most widely read newspapers in the region, he had a platform from which to promote his work. This, in a town which was not exactly overflowing with literary talent, resulted in his attracting a circle of syncopatic admirers willing to hang on to his every word. Few modern anthologies of poetry carry any of his work, although some of his hymns are still sung on occasions.

Apart from his statue, there is a drinking fountain dedicated to his memory in Broad Lane. This bears the legend, now almost unreadable, "Rest For The Weary". It was later converted to a street lamp. Also, The Montgomery Theatre, a hall cum theatre building in Surrey Street and several streets are also named after him.

SAMUEL HOLBERRY

Samuel Holberry, depending from which angle you view his life, was either a working class martyr or a trouble making rabble rouser. His name is still able to raise a certain amount of emotion in both camps, although perhaps not as strongly as might have been thought at the time of his death in 1842. In several books written about the Chartist movement, his name is not prominently featured.

He was born the youngest of nine children in Gamston, near Retford, Nottinghamshire on November 18th, 1814 and died on June 21st, 1842. His father, John, was someone very near to the bottom of the social pile, spending his life working as an agricultural labourer on the estate of the Duke of Newcastle. Samuel had a miserable childhood, as was common with his class during this period. His father would have received little more than bare subsistence wages with which to bring up his large family with little or no hope of improvement.

Barely educated, Holberry spent most of his formative years working on the land until, desperate to escape a life steeped in grinding poverty, boredom and want, at 17 years old and under age, he enlisted in the Army and joined the 33rd Regiment of Foot. It was not an unusual thing for a boy of his background to do.

He served for three years, most of which time was spent in England, although he was for a spell in Ireland. Strangely, at that time he appears to have been a confirmed loyalist and joined the ultra conservative Protestant Orange Lodge which was popular in the Army at that time. He spent much of his Army service admiring the masters that he was later to despise and oppose.

After a period when he attended night school in Northampton, he became better educated and literate enough to be able to recognise and consider the political situation of the day and the radical tradition of the Northampton cobblers, with whom he associated, convinced him that their politics was the road to follow. He borrowed enough money to purchase his discharge from the Army and returned home in 1835.

He arrived in Sheffield and worked first for a cooper and then for a firm of distillers where he learned the trade of rectifying distiller before being laid off in 1837.

It was about this time that the first meeting of the Sheffield Workingmans' Association was held. This was the first local Chartist organisation and it pledged, " to obtain universal sufferage, payment of MP's, the abolition of the property owning requirements of MP's, secret ballots and equality in the size of parliamentary constituencies".

Holberry, unemployed in Sheffield, went to London to seek work, where he became heavily involved in the Chartist movement and, after a year there, he returned to Sheffield and joined the Sheffield Chartists.

In 1839, Holberry was at the forefront of all the Chartist activities in the north of England, which culminated in the botched attempt to seize control of Sheffield by force on the night of January 11/12th, 1840. Many of the conspirators were betrayed and both Holberry and his wife were among those arrested.

Holberry's wife was later released without charge, but Holberry and seven of his fellow plotters were indicted to appear at the York Spring Assizes on March 16th, 1840 to answer charges of high treason - charges which carrried the death penalty.

He was, however, found guilty of the lesser charge of seditious conspiracy and sentenced to four years imprisonment in the Northallerton House of Correction. Although his sentence did not include hard labour and suffering increasingly from ill health due to consumption, he was forced to spend five weeks on the soul and backbreaking treadmill and was also in solitary confinement for several months.

In spite of numerous petitions for clemency from all over the country, Holberry died in York Hospital at 4.30am on June 21st, 1842.

The Headstone of Samuel Holberry in the General Cemetery

When his body was returned to Sheffield and the funeral procession passed through the streets of the city, from Attercliffe to the new General Cemetery, Ecclesall Road, a route of over two miles, about 50,000 people turned out to line the route.

The grave of Samuel Holberry can still be seen in the General Cemetery. It is in the midst of a great crowded collection of other tombstones, but its popularity can be judged by the well trodden path through the long grass which leads up to his stone.

The Sheffield Chartists had a bust made of Holberry and it was kept in the National Charter Association Rooms until the 1850's, when it was removed to storage in a workshop. It is at the moment being cared for by The Friends of the General Cemetery.

Samuel Holberry is now largely forgotten, apart from a small metal plaque which was attached to one of the concrete pillars supporting the front of the new town hall extension. This was recently removed to allow for development and demolition works. It will, no doubt, be eventually displayed somewhere else in the vacinity.

Today, all the demands made by the 19th century Chartists have been achieved. Perhaps this would be of consolation to Samuel Holberry - to know that he had been right all along.

The inscription on Samuel Holberry's
tombstone reads:-

SACRED
TO THE MEMORY OF
SAMUEL HOLBERRY
WHO AT THE EARLY AGE OF 27 DIED
IN YORK CASTLE, AFTER SUFFERING
AN IMPRISONMENT OF TWO YEARS AND THREE
MONTHS, JUNE 21st 1842.
FOR ADVOCATING WHAT TO HIM APPEARED,
TO BE THE TRUE INTEREST OF THE PEOPLE OF
ENGLAND.
THIS TABLET WAS ERECTED BY HIS BEREFT WIDOW.

THE CASEY FAMILY

This grave is in the churchyard of All Saints Church in Ecclesall. It has several points of interest engraved on it. Firstly, Annie Casey was a local preacher for 53 of her 69 years; secondly, her husband Thomas was both a Justice of the Peace and a Member of Parliament and thirdly, Private Casey, the son of Annie and Thomas, was killed on the first day of the Battle of the Somme. The City Battalion was often referred to as the Pals Battalion. Pte. Casey, who was serving as part of the 31st Division, was killed at Serre, which was part of the 20 mile long front which was attacked on that day. Most of the large towns and cities in Britain raised at least one of these volunteer battalions. Many of the men who served in them were well known to each other and some were actually from the same streets or worked together. These battalions of eager young men paid a fearful toll for their patriotic eagerness in lost lives, maimed bodies and minds.

The death of Mrs Casey is reported in the Sheffield Daily Telegraph in the issue dated 6th July, 1931:-

"Following an operation at Skegness,
Mrs Casey, of 61 Bents Rd, Sheffield, wife of
Mr TW Casey, who is well known in Trade Union
circles as general secretary of the National Winding
and General Engineers' Society, and was formerly Member of
Parliament for Attercliffe, died on Saturday.
Mrs Casey, who was 69 years of age, went to
Sutton on Sea for health reasons some weeks ago.
A women of considerable talents, Mrs Casey had a wide experience
of religious work, and was an effective platform speaker.
Before her marriage she lived in Annesley Woodhouse, Nottingham,
and was an evangelist for the Methodist Free Church. She commenced
her activities in this direction at the age of sixteen.
During her long residence in Sheffield, Mrs TW Casey actively
associated herself with religious work in various parts of the city. At one
time she was connected with Petre Street Chapel, and with Greystones
Primitive Methodist Church. Mrs Casey was a Citizen Association
member of the City Council for Attercliffe."

Her husband, Thomas Casey also rated an obituary in the Sheffield Daily Telegraph. It is dated the day after his death, November 30th, 1949:-

"Mr T.W. Casey, a former MP for the Attercliffe Division of Sheffield,
and a local magistrate until two years ago, died at his home at
61, Bents Rd, Sheffield, yesterday at the age of 80. Mr Casey, who was
born at Intake, Sheffield, started work on a farm at the age of 12, and a
year later went to Birley Colliery.
At the age of 18 he went to Cadeby Colliery, near Rotherham, as a
winding engineman. He became president and later general secretary
of the National Winding and General Engineers' Society.
He was elected Coalition Liberal - Labour candidate for Attercliffe,
and represented the division from 1918 to 1922. He was also for six
years a member of Mexborough Council, and was well known as a
Methodist lay preacher. Mr Casey, who was married twice, leaves behind a
widow and two daughters.
The funeral service will take place at Bents Green Methodist Church
on December 2, at 11.0 a.m."

On the gravestone after Mr Casey's name are the letters M.P. These were only added recently while the stone was being repaired following an attack by vandals.

SACRED TO THE MEMORY OF
ANNIE
THE BELOVED WIFE OF
THOMAS W. CASEY JP.MP,
WHO PASSED OVER JULY 4th 1931
AGED 69 YEARS
AN EVANGELIST AND LOCAL PREACHER
OF THE GOSPEL FOR 53 YEARS.
THOMAS W. CASEY JP. MP.
BORN 13th OCT. 1869.
DIED 29th NOV. 1949.
AND THEIR DAUGHTER
EUNICE ANNIE CASEY
BORN 14th DEC. 1889 - DIED 21st JULY 1935.
SACRED TO THE MEMORY OF
PRIVATE ALPHEAUS A. CASEY.
12th YORK & LANCASTER REG.
(CITY BATTALION)
SON OF THE ABOVE WHO FELL IN ACTION
SOMEWHERE IN FRANCE
JULY 1st 1916 AGED 21 YEARS.

TWO FROM THE TOWN HALL

The following two memorials are to local politicians. The first one can be found just at the start of Tinsley Park Cemetery, behind the twin buildings which dominate the entrance.

The name of John Charles Whiteley is practically unknown today, but in his time he was a high profile and contentious political activist in Sheffield.

Born without any privilege to speak of, he was working in a brickyard at 10 years old, then at 11 years old he was a riveter's labourer in a boilermakers workshop. From there, for this ambitious boy, the only way was up.

He grew up fast and by the time he was 22 years old, he was the president of the Rotherham Branch of the Steam Engine Maker's Society. He had been born in the Park area of Sheffield, his parents had moved out to live at Masborough when he was a child and, as a young man, when Whiteley moved back to Sheffield, he quickly became embroiled in the politics of the working classes. He became the official Liberal Agent for Attercliffe from 1870 - 1878, meanwhile educating himself during what spare time he had.

He was elected Liberal councillor for Attercliffe in 1895 and was the member for this area until his death in 1911. His radical views and strong expression of them and his other opinions often brought conflict with the leader of the party, Sir William Clegg, and his obituary in the Sheffield Independent described him as, "a radical reformer of the old school".

He gave his views on the emerging Socialists as follows, "If you ask me if I am a Socialist who believes in placing in the hands of the Community all the means of production, distribution and exchange, I should say that I regarded it as a great ideal to place before the public, but all selfishness in human nature would have to be eradicated before such a system could succeed".

His memorial is a square pillar which is engraved as follows:-

JOHN CHARLES WHITELEY
DIED 9th OCTOBER, 1911
CITY COUNCILLOR FOR
ATTERCLIFFE
FROM 1895 TO 1911
HE GAVE HIS LIFE
FOR THE PEOPLE
ERECTED AS A TRIBUTE
OF PUBLIC AFFECTION

The second memorial can be seen in the old Attercliffe Cemetery. This cemetery is quite large, but has only a sparse number of tombstones which are widely spread across the area. Between the graveyard and Attercliffe Road there is a small garden surrounded by tombstones and this is where Christ Church used to stand. This tomb is a large obelisk with engraving on three sides. It is badly stained and darkened by the pollution which used to be the price the area had to pay for the existence of the vast, greedy and filthy steelworks which were for so long the lifeblood of this part of the Don Valley.

ERECTED
BY PUBLIC SUBSCRIPTION
TO THE MEMORY OF THE LATE
RALPH SKELTON
WHO FOR 15 YEARS FULLY SERVED
THE RATEPAYERS OF THE TOWNSHIP OF
ATTERCLIFFE CUM DARNALL IN THE TOWN COUNCIL
OF THE BOROUGH OF SHEFFIELD AND IDENTIFIED
HIMSELF WITH EVERY LOCAL MOVEMENT FOR THE
PUBLIC GOOD FOR UPWARDS OF 25 YEARS
HIS STERLING WORTH GAINED FOR HIM THE ESTEEM
AND RESPECT OF ALL

(this is on the front of the obelisk)

BORN 12th AUGUST 1815

(this is on one side of the obelisk)

DIED 17th MAY 1877

(this is on the other side of the obelisk)

There follows a copy of the obituary which was published in the Sheffield Daily Telegraph on May 18th, 1877:-

"Death of Mr Councillor Skelton - We regret to announce the death of Mr Councillor Skelton, who expired at one o'clock yesterday afternoon. The deceased gentleman had been ill for about a year, his disorder having originated from sleeping in a damp bed. At Christmas paralysis attacked his left side, and on Saturday he had a second stroke, which has proved fatal in its results. Mr Skelton was elected in 1863 to represent Attercliffe Ward in the Town Council and was thus in his fifteenth year as a councillor."

CHAPTER TWO

THE CRUEL COST OF COAL

"Coal-black and grizzled here and there,
But more through toil than age."
Sir Walter Scott
1771-1832

THERE are, scattered throughout certain graveyards in the city, the tombstones which serve as monuments to the miners who were killed in the coal mines. These mines once scarred the landscape around the east and northern areas of Sheffield, but ugly as they might have been, they provided both a living for many of the local men and the means to produce great wealth for the steel works.

All these mines are now closed, many of them long ago, and almost all of them are forgotten, the traces left behind by this savage business smoothed away by modern progress and development. The grave stones which remain are the sole reminder of the awful price exacted and levied in human lives, which has always had to be paid by the men who spent their working hours wresting the "black gold" from the earth in order to keep Sheffield's industrial heart beating so profitably for so long.

There are easy jobs and there are difficult and dangerous jobs, but few jobs are overshadowed by the ever present spectre of sudden death somewhere deep in the earth.

There isn't a huge number of these graves - Sheffield, unlike other areas of the old West Riding, has never been a large producer of coal, but there are more than enough.

The following graves are in several areas around Chapeltown, Brightside and Tinsley. The dates span almost 100 years. The following two graves are in Tinsley Park Cemetery.

IN LOVING MEMORY OF
WILLIAM
THE BELOVED HUSBAND
OF
ANNIE GELSTHORPE
WHO WAS FATALLY
INJURED AT
TINSLEY PARK COLLIERY
NOVer 24th
DIED NOVer 29th 1908 AGED
21 YEARS

I have searched all the local newspapers, but have been unable to find any mention of this accident.

A newspaper report on the following accident, taken from The Sheffield & Rotherham Independent, Monday, July 30th, 1894, reads in part:-

FATAL COLLIERY ACCIDENT AT HEMSWORTH

"On Saturday afternoon Major Taylor, JP., held an inquest at the Clayton Hospital, at Wakefield, on the body of John Radford, 18 years of age, who had lived with his parents at No. 49, Fitzwilliam Terrace, Tinsley. The deceased was employed at the Hemsworth Fitzwilliam Colliery, and on Friday afternoon he was attending to his duties when he was accidentally crushed by the cage. He was placed in the ambulance and whilst being removed to Clayton Hospital he expired. The verdict:- accidentally killed. "

JOHN, THE BELOVED SON OF THE ABOVE
(George & Mary Radford)
WHO LOST HIS LIFE AT THE HEMSWORTH
COLLIERY, JULY 27th 1894

This grave in Ecclesfield Churchyard contains the remains of some of the Jeffcock family, who have had a lengthy history in the Sheffield area.

The most recent history of this family stems from John Jeffcock (1763 - 1814), who had four sons. William was born in 1800 and was a coalmaster and partner in various collieries around the Handsworth area of Sheffield. He lived in High Hazels House and was the first mayor of Sheffield in 1843 and also a Justice of the Peace, appointed in 1846.

He died in Dunmoyle, Co. Tyrone on November 21st, 1871 and was buried in Handsworth Churchyard. A portrait of him, which was painted in 1867 by HF Crichton, and repainted in 1877 after it fell off the wall in the town hall council chamber, still hangs there.

His brother, John, second son of John Jeffcock Snr, lived at Cowley Hall in Ecclesfield; he was born in 1803 and died in 1878. He was also a Justice of the Peace and was buried in the grave pictured.

John's son, Parkin Jeffcock, also buried in the grave, is probably the most famous of a family which is becoming forgotten. He was born on October 27th, 1829 and was articled in 1850 to George Hunter, a colliery viewer and engineer. He made rapid progress in his profession and in 1857, he became a partner of JT Woodhouse, a mining engineer and agent in Derby. In 1861, he distinguished himself by trying to save the lives of the men and boys who were trapped in a coal mine at Clay Cross following what was described as an "inundation". This was the usual 19th century word for flooding.

Jeffcock Family Grave

On December 12th, 1866, he was informed that the Oaks Pit, near Barnsley, was on fire. He went there at once and, with a team of others, went inside the mine to make a complete exploration of the situation. While they were below, a second explosion ripped through the mine and Parkin Jeffcock and all but one of his group of volunteers were killed.

The colliery was sealed off to avoid further loss of life and it was not until October 5th, 1867, that his body was recovered. The total death toll for this tragic mining disaster was 348 men and boys and 40 pit ponies. Despite lengthy, desperate and determined efforts, about 100 of the bodies were never recovered and remain where they fell to this day.

News of this huge mining tragedy reached the front pages of all the national newspapers and Parkin Jeffcock has his own place in the Dictionary of National Biography.

In his memory and using money from his memorial fund, the church of St. Saviour's was built in his memory at Mortomley. This huge investment of both money and labour indicates just how impressed his fellow townspeople were with his bravery.

There is also a horse trough in Ecclesfield churchyard and a drinking fountain in Ecclesfield Park in memory of the Jeffcocks; also a combined drinking fountain and horse trough just before the churchyard in Handsworth, by the Turf Tavern.

Due to the fact that three of the four sons of the original John Jeffcock lived near to Handsworth Churchyard, many of the old family are buried in a large family plot and vault there. The remainder of this family seem for the most part to be buried in Ecclesfield Churchyard.

I have only recorded part of the inscription on this large, damaged and rather weatherbeaten grave.

PARKIN JEFFCOCK
LATE OF PARKIN IN THE COUNTY OF DERBY
ESQUIRE, CIVIL ENGINEER
NEPHEW OF THE SAID WILLIAM PARKIN
AND SECOND CHILD AND ELDEST SON OF
JOHN AND KATHERINE JEFFCOCK
OF COWLEY MANOR, IN THIS PARISH
WHERE HE WAS BORN OCTOBER 27th 1829
HE DIED IN THE GREAT EXPLOSION AT THE
OAKS COLLIERY, NEAR BARNSLEY LEADING
A BAND OF VOLUNTEER EXPLORERS
DECEMBER 13th 1866 AND WAS BURIED HERE
OCTOBER 7th 1867

This grave is in St. Thomas's Churchyard, Grimesthorpe. The following record of the accident was in The Sheffield & Rotherham Independent dated Saturday, 25th January, 1873:-

THE SAD ACCIDENT AT GRIMESTHORPE COLLIERY

"The funeral of the unfortunate man, William Mannifield, an overman at the Brightside Colliery, who was killed there on Monday, took place a day or so since. The deceased appears to have been much respected, for his body was followed to its last resting place by 600 of his fellow workmen and others. In the evening a meeting took place at The Station Inn, Brightside, when a committee was appointed to receive subscriptions for the purpose of erecting a monument over the deceased's grave."

THIS STONE WAS ERECTED
BY THE FRIENDS
AND FELLOW WORKMEN,
IN AFFECTIONATE REMEMBERANCE OF
WILLIAM MANNIFIELD,
WHO WAS ACCIDENTALLY KILLED,
AT BRIGHTSIDE COLLIERY, JAN. 20th 1873,
AGED 40 YEARS.
A SUDDEN CHANGE, HE IN A MOMENT FELL,
HE HAD NOT TIME TO BID HIS FRIENDS
FAREWELL,
THINK IT NOT STRANGE, DEATH HAPPENS
UNTO ALL,
TODAY WE LIVE, TOMORROW WE MAY FALL.

All the following graves may be found in Burncross Cemetery, Chapeltown.

IN LOVING MEMORY OF
HENRY
THE LOVED HUSBAND OF
MAY COOPER
WHO WAS ACCIDENTALLY KILLED AT BARROW
COLLy JANy 7th 1932, AGED 46 YEARS

This man met an awful death. It was reported on Tuesday, January, 12th, 1932, in The Sheffield Daily Telegraph:-

TRAGEDY IN MINE

FELL ONTO COAL - CUTTING MACHINE

"A High Green man's terrible death after a fall on to a coal-cutting machine was investigated at the inquest at Barnsley, yesterday, on Henry Cooper (46), a coal-cutting machine attendant, of 142, Thompson Hill, High Green.

Joseph William Pinder, Potter Hill, High Green, said Cooper was holding a derrick rail and shouted, "Right," so witness put the machine in motion. The rail slipped, and Cooper and another man shouted, "Whoa," and witness cut off the air.

"The rail slipped," witness went on, "and Cooper lost his balance and turned a somersault over the machine. He was caught by the picks, which had not stopped moving although the air was turned off. They were just slowing down. They did not stop instantly."

Answering the Inspector of Mines (Mr G. W. Scott) witness said a fall of dirt had interfered with a spring on the lever, otherwise the picks would have stopped sooner.

The jury returned a verdict of, "death by misadventure", and suggested that certain points raised should be considered with a view to preventing similar accidents."

IN LOVING MEMORY OF
WILLIAM
THE BELOVED HUSBAND OF
NELLIE FISHER
WHO WAS ACCIDENTALLY KILLED IN THE
WHARNCLIFFE SILKSTONE COLLIERY
EXPLOSION, MAY 30th 1914
AGED 32 YEARS.
BE YE ALSO READY, FOR IN EACH AN HOUR AS
YE THINK NOT THE SON OF MAN COMETH.
ALSO EDWARD FISHER
THEIR BELOVED SON
WHO WAS ACCIDENTALLY KILLED
IN THE HARWORTH COLLIERY
JULY 10th 1928 AGED 15 YEARS.

There are two newspaper accounts of these miners' deaths - 14 years apart. The first one is dated 30th May, 1914, taken from The Sheffield Daily Independent and is heavily edited as the account was very large in keeping with the magnitude of the disaster:-

"Eleven men were killed and two were severely injured in an explosion of gas in the Wharncliffe Silkstone Colliery on Saturday afternoon. It is the first big disaster at Wharncliffe Silkstone.

Coal cutters worked by electricity were being used in the explosion zone at the time.

Several men had miraculous escapes. One named Fisher, who was badly injured, had practically given himself up for lost when he was discovered by his fleeing comrades and helped to the pit bottom."

This final piece of the report was optimistic for William Fisher died soon afterwards.

The second account, concerning his son, Edward, comes from the same newspaper, dated Monday, 16th July, 1928:-

"The internment took place on Saturday at Chapeltown of Edward Fisher (15), who was killed in the Harworth Colliery, near Doncaster. He was buried in the same grave as his father, the late Mr William Fisher, of High Green, who was killed in the Wharncliffe Silkstone Colliery explosion in 1914."

IN LOVING MEMORY OF
HORACE GLADWIN
THE BELOVED HUSBAND OF
HILDA DENTON
WHO WAS ACCIDENTALLY KILLED
AT THORNCLIFFE COLLIERY
FEBy 28th 1933, AGED 31 YEARS
IN THE MIDST OF LIFE WE ARE IN DEATH

MAN ELECTROCUTED IN MINE

WITNESS SUGGESTS RATS HAD GNAWED CABLE

"Rats gnawing the insulation of an electric cable, from which a man received a fatal shock, was the theory advanced by a witness at the Chapeltown inquest yesterday on Horace Gladwin Denton, aged 31, of 17 Warren Hill, Chapeltown coal-cutter and machine-man.

Denton was killed on Tuesday in the new Silkstone Pit of Messrs. Newton Chambers & Co.....

......Arthur Marshall, electrician, of Park View Rd, Chapeltown, said the abrasion on the cable looked like the result of a rat gnawing it. He said he had chased rats off the cable himself. They attacked the insulation - the portion they could eat - and his suggestion was quite serious.

A verdict of accidental death was recorded."

This account of the inquest is taken from The Sheffield Daily Independent, Friday, 3rd March, 1933.

This account, also from The Sheffield Daily Independent dated Tuesday, 5th August, 1930, shows just how unlucky were the Morley family:-

FOURTH SUDDEN DEATH IN FAMILY

"The funeral took place yesterday at Chapeltown of Mr Ernest Morley (50), of Greenland Lane, Chapeltown, who was killed last Thursday while working at Thorncliffe Colliery.

One of his brothers was killed seven years ago at Tinsley Park Colliery, and another brother died in hospital from injuries received at the same colliery.

Their father, who worked on the railway, was also killed at work. "

IN LOVING MEMORY OF
ERNEST
THE DEARLY BELOVED HUSBAND OF
EMILY MORLEY
WHO WAS ACCIDENTALLY KILLED AT THE
THORNCLIFFE COLLIERIES JULY 31st 1930
AGED 50 YEARS
IN THE MIDST OF LIFE WE ARE IN DEATH
ALSO EMILY
DIED NOVr 5 1915, AGED 11 MONTHS
ALSO ANNIE
DIED OCTr 25th 1918, AGED 5 YEARS
ALSO THE ABOVE NAMED
EMILY MORLEY
DIED JULY 26th 1946 AGED 65 YEARS
REUNITED

By the age of about 50, Emily Morley had suffered more than her share of grief.

An account from The Star, Thursday, May 13th, 1965:-

HIGH GREEN MAN KILLED BY ROPE

"A 44 year old High Green man was killed last night when he was struck by a shearer rope at Wharncliffe Silkstone Colliery, near Barnsley.

He was Eric Howarth, a ripper, of Miles Rd. An N.C.B. spokesman at Doncaster said that Mr Howarth was working in the old Fenton One seam at the colliery when he was killed. He leaves a widow and three children - two still at school.

An inquest will be opened on Mr Howarth tomorrow at Grenoside.

Mr Howarth worked in collieries for over 20 years, and moved to this section of Silkstone eight months ago."

IN LOVING MEMORY OF ERIC HOWARTH
DEARLY BELOVED HUSBAND OF MARY
LOVING FATHER OF JOY, CAROL & KEITH
ACCIDENTALLY KILLED MAY 12 1965
AT WHARNCLIFFE SILKSTONE COLLIERY
AGED 44 YEARS

This is a part inscription taken from the Bond family grave:-

...ALSO GEORGE
THE BELOVED SON OF THE ABOVE
WHO WAS ACCIDENTALLY KILLED AT
THORPE NEW PIT JUNE 11th 1925
AGED 48 YEARS
IN THE MIDST OF LIFE WE ARE IN DEATH

This account of the accident is taken from The Sheffield Daily Independent dated June 12th, 1925:-

TWO MEN KILLED
FALL OF ROOF AT THORPE HESLEY PIT

"James Richards, married, of Green Head, Chapeltown, and George Bond, single, of Warren ....?, Chapeltown, were killed by a fall of roof which occured in Smithywood Colliery, Thorpe Hesley, yesterday.
The mishap occurred about 4o'clock in the afternoon and the men mentioned and two or three other men were together at a spot about eight minutes walk from the pit bottom.
An iron girder sprang out of position, releasing other girders, and a heavy fall followed."

Although the man remembered on the gravestone below was not named as a coal miner, there was a small, three line mention of his death in the Sheffield Daily Telegraph on the 21st September, 1920:-

"Harry Holland, (a) married man, of Utley Street, Darnall, was killed by a fall of roof at Tinsley Pit yesterday afternoon."

IN LOVING MEMORY OF HARRY,
THE BELOVED HUSBAND OF
ALICE HOLLAND,
WHO WAS ACCIDENTALLY KILLED
SEPT. 20th 1920,
AGED 41 YEARS.
GONE BUT NOT FORGOTTEN.

Also mentioned on the stone is Alice, who was 86 years old

The cemetery at Intake is situated just off Mansfield Road, on the way to Mosborough. From the road it seems to be merely a few graves and a small chapel, but once inside the gates the large number of graves which are hidden from the road by the slope of the land may be seen. The chapel, as is usual in Sheffield, is only used now by the council workmen, who tend the cemetery so well, as a store for their machinery. It is a shame that this architecturally unremarkable, but attractive little building can't be used for the purpose it was built.

These coal miners' graves are in Intake Cemetery; two of them were killed at Orgreave Colliery. I have been unable to find any information regarding the first man's death.

IN CHERISHED
REMEMBERANCE OF
JOHN HENRY,
THE BELOVED HUSBAND OF
AMY ASLIN VERNON,
WHO DIED ON DECEMBER 11th 1927,
FROM INJURIES RECEIVED
AT ORGREAVE COLLIERY,
AGED 53 YEARS.

The following two graves are very close to each other and, although I have no proof of this, the similarity between these surnames seems to show that they were related. If this is so, then both father and son of the Porter family were killed in coal mining accidents. I have not been able to find an account of the death of Ronald Porter, but the account of Frederick Porter's death is from The Sheffield Daily Independent, Monday, 14th July, 1924:-

KILLED IN THE PIT: WOODHOUSE MINER CRUSHED BY FALL

"A fall of roof, at the Birley East Pit, Woodhouse, on Friday, resulted in the death of Fred Porter (32), of 44 Victoria Rd, Woodhouse.

A verdict of "accidental death" was returned at the inquest on Saturday. The widow stated that her husband had worked at the coalface for over ten years.

Albert Haslam, of 6 Britton Hill, Handsworth, a workmate of Porter's, said that at about 9pm he heard a bump and a groan, and then discovered that Porter was pinned underneath a fall of rock. When he was got out the man was dead.

The roof had been examined in the morning and then appeared to be quite secure and well timbered. There was no sign of a break.

An assistant at the mortuary, Harold Hudson, stated that the body was badly crushed, and the spine was fractured."

ALSO OF FREDERICK,
THE BELOVED HUSBAND OF ELSIE PORTER,
WHO WAS ACCIDENTALLY KILLED
AT BIRLEY EAST PIT
JULY 11th 1924, AGED 32 YEARS.
A LOVING HUSBAND AND FATHER
SOMEDAY WE'LL UNDERSTAND

IN LOVING MEMORY OF RONALD
THE DEARLY LOVED SON OF
FRED & ELSIE PORTER,
WHO WAS ACCIDENTALLY KILLED AT
ORGREAVE COLLIERY JUNE 12th 1942,
AGED 21 YEARS. "LOVED BY ALL."

CHAPTER THREE

IT WAS AN ACCIDENT.....!

" Oh, then indulge thy grief, nor fear to tell,
the gentle source from whence thy sorrows flow..."
William Cowper
1731-1800

TO DIE through illness or old age is something which everyone accepts as one of the facts of life; a truth which has to be faced eventually by us all. It is what happens and is inevitable. But to die by accident? Well, that is something for which there can be no preparation, no readiness. It is a hideous severing of a life before its natural end and as such makes the event, for those left to mourn, all the harder to bear. If only, if only....! The thought never goes away.

The very phrase, "by accident", meaning whatever happened was unplanned, by chance, unintentional or bad luck, seems to me to be the most cruel way of all for a life to end.

It doesn't take much for a simple mistake to be transformed into a tragedy. A split second, perhaps, of inattention; cutting a corner when doing a dangerous job, to save time or to earn a few more pence, or worst of all, being the victim of someone else's blunder. Just to be in the wrong place at the wrong time is sometimes enough.

Fatal accidents have always happened, especially since life stopped being a simple matter of survival and mankind began to think and to develop upwards from a superior ape into an inventive and intelligent human being. And, as life and living become ever more complex, then so do the ways by which fatal accidents can occur.

Plenty of lives were lost to accidents in the years preceding this century and that was before the advent of electricity, powerful engines and the aeroplane. Plus thousands of other new inventions which make life easier to live and also to lose.

Here is a selection of the graves of people who have lost their lives through accidents; they are often fairly young. This group of three are in Burncross Cemetery:-

IN LOVING MEMORY OF
LEONARD AND RUTH WINKLEY
(AGED 46 & 45 YEARS)
AND THEIR ELDER SON
MICHAEL (17 YEARS)
DIED, TOGETHER IN A ROAD
ACCIDENT IN FRANCE
AUGUST 10th 1965
HAPPY THE SOULS
TO JESUS JOINED

This report is from The Sheffield Telegraph, Wednesday, August 11th, 1965:-

TRAGEDY ON FAMILY'S FIRST TRIP ABROAD

"Three members of a Nottingham family travelling to their first holiday abroad were killed on their first day on the Continent, when their car was in collision with a lorry near Paris last night.

They were Mr and Mrs Leonard Winkley, both aged about 45, of Wroxham Drive, Nottingham and their eldest son, Michael, aged 18. Another son, nine year old Nigel, was taken to hospital seriously injured.

Last night police were trying to trace relatives and were making enquiries in the Sheffield area. It is believed Mr and Mrs Winkley both came from the Chapeltown area."

IN LOVING MEMORY OF
SHEILA
THE DEARLY LOVED DAUGHTER OF
CHARLES & MIRIAM WILSDON
WHO WAS ACCIDENTALLY KILLED
APRIL 11th 1947
AGED 14½ YEARS
IN HEAVENLY LOVE ABIDING

This is an edited newspaper report:-

"Two girls cycling home from work last night were killed in Chapeltown in a crash with a car on the main Sheffield to Barnsley Road. They were Miss Irene Hayward, aged 23, and Miss Sheila Wilsdon, aged 14. Their two companions were treated for injuries, but allowed home.

An eye-witness report said that the car turned a treble somersault before coming to rest with Miss Hayward pinned beneath with her cycle. She was dead when extricated. Miss Wilsdon died within minutes."

IN LOVING MEMORY OF WALTER THE BELOVED
SON OF WALTER AND KATE TEASDALE
WHO DIED JUNE 29th 1923 AGED 10 YEARS
ALSO STANLEY THEIR SON ACCIDENTALLY
KILLED AT THORNCLIFFE IRONWORKS
MAY 15th 1941 AGED 20 YEARS
IN THE MIDST OF LIFE WE ARE IN DEATH

As this accident happened during the Second World War, for security reasons the name of the company who owned the factory were not named. This edited report is taken from The Sheffield Telegraph & Independent, Friday, 16th May, 1941:-

FOUR KILLED IN WORKSHOP EXPLOSION

"Four men were killed and several others were treated for shock when an explosion occurred at a workshop near Sheffield yesterday.
The four killed were:- CH Thompson (41) manager of the shop; Fred Furniss (51), the foreman; William Watkinson (24); and Stanley Teasdale (20).
They were blown through the roof of the shop which was 20 feet high. The bodies of three were recovered from the roof and the other was found across a road 40 ft away."

The cause of this accident was said to have been the explosion of an acetylene welding bottle.

These two graves can be seen in Tinsley Park Cemetery. In both cases, I have been unable to find newspaper reports to flesh out the stark inscriptions on the gravestones.

WILLIAM BENNETT
THE DEARLY BELOVED HUSBAND
OF ANNIE ELIZABETH JOHNSON
WHO WAS ACCIDENTALLY KILLED
JULY 25th 1911
WHILST FOLLOWING HIS
EMPLOYMENT AT
Wm COOKE & Co WORKS TINSLEY
AGED 28 YEARS

THE COST OF THIS MEMORIAL WAS DEFRAYED
BY PUBLIC SUBSCRIPTIONS IN RECOGNITION
OF A BRAVE DEED NOBLY DONE
IN MEMORY OF GEORGE, SON OF MARGARET
AND THE LATE WILLIAM CLARKE, AGED 19
YEARS WHO BRAVELY SACRIFICED HIS LIFE IN
ATTEMPTING TO SAVE A YOUTH FROM
DROWNING IN THE ATTERCLIFFE CANAL,
SEPTEMBER 4th, 1902

This grave is in Attercliffe Cemetery. As the only normal form of transport in and around 1875 was the horse, or walking, it is surprising that more people weren't killed in their dealings with them. This is a newspaper report on his death:-

A BOY KICKED TO DEATH IN SHEFFIELD

"A fatal accident happened yesterday afternoon to a lad about 19 years old named William Henry Parker. It seemed that the deceased was an errand boy employed by Mr Lee, confectioner, Sheffield Moor, whose grey pony he usually rode. Between four and five yesterday afternoon he had occasion to go into Burgess Street and seeing some lads standing near a workshop and dismounted to speak to them. He led the pony into a yard and began to tease it, the pony kicked him in the breast with great force knocking him down. The other lads, noticing that he lay quite still, raised him up and found he was dead. A medical gentleman was sent for, but his services were to no avail. He said that the kick most probably had driven the breast bone into the heart, thereby causing instantaneous death. The body was removed to The Reuben's Head, Cross Burgess Street where it awaits a coroner's inquest."

WILLIAM HENRY
SON OF WILLIAM
AND JANE PARKER
WHO WAS KILLED BY A KICK FROM A
HORSE OCTr 7th 1875 AGED 19 YEARS
" DEATH NO WARNING TO ME GAVE
BUT TOOK ME QUICKLY TO MY GRAVE
READER BOAST NOT OF THY MIGHT
ALIVE AT NOON AND DEAD AT NIGHT"

This grave, in Ecclesfield Churchyard, is one of several that I have found concerning death on the railways. This edited report is from The Sheffield & Rotherham Independent dated December 13th, 1870:-

TERRIBLE RAILWAY ACCIDENT NEAR BARNSLEY

"A terrible collision occurred at Stairfoot Station, near Barnsley, on the Manchester, Sheffield & Lincolnshire Railway last night, by which fourteen passengers were killed and more than twenty seriously injured. Shortly after six o'clock in the evening, a number of goods trucks which were being shunted on a siding in the vicinity of Barnsley Station got loose and ran down the incline to Stairfoot, a distance of two miles. The train from Sheffield to Barnsley had just drawn up at Stairfoot Station, and the goods trucks ran into it with fearful violence, smashing the break-van (sic) and two passenger carriages. The consequences were dreadful."

At the lengthy inquest which followed on December 15th, 1870, the jury said that in their opinion John Heathershaw, a railway employee, was guilty of manslaughter. He was committed for trial and allowed bail.

IN MEMORY OF
GEORGE HORSFIELD
OF BURN CROSS, NEAR CHAPELTOWN
WHO WAS KILLED BY THE RAILWAY
ACCIDENT AT ARDSLEY, NEAR BARNSLEY
DECEMBER 12th 1870 IN HIS 29th YEAR

The following graves are in Shiregreen Cemetery and are a matched pair made of black marble with identical surrounds. The inscriptions bear witness to a tragedy which occured in 1965. It is always a sobering thought that young people, carefree and adventurous, can end their lives so suddenly.

This report is from The Sheffield Telegraph, Monday July 12th, 1965:

"A 15 year old girl and her boyfrined, aged 18, died on Saturday night when their motorcycle and a taxi crashed in Shirecliffe Rd, Shirecliffe. David Milton Richards, of Herries Rd, was driving Christine Weston to her home in Crumpsall Rd for a party to celebrate her 16th birthday. The machine was thrown 10 feet into the air. The couple were trapped under the wheels of the taxi and were dead when firemen released them. After the accident, police measured a pothole in the road and yesterday morning the hole had been filled in."

A TRIBUTE OF LOVE
TO OUR DEAR DAUGHTER
CHRISTINE WESTON,
TRAGICALLY KILLED JULY 10th 1965,
AGED 15 YEARS.

(This is the inscription on the left hand grave)

A TRIBUTE OF LOVE
TO OUR DEAR SON
DAVID MILTON RICHARDS,
TRAGICALLY KILLED JULY 10th 1965,
AGED 18 YEARS.

(This is the inscription on the right hand grave)

The following graves are in Intake Cemetery, Mansfield Road. These three graves remember young people who were killed in accidents.

ALSO MYRA DOROTHEA,
THEIR ELDER DAUGHTER,
WHO WAS CALLED HOME BY FATAL
MACHINERY ACCIDENT, WHILST
EMPLOYED AS A LANDGIRL
AT SOUTH FARM, LETWELL, YORKS.
DECr 7th 1920, AGED 24 YEARS.

This report is taken from the December 9th, 1920 edition of The Sheffield Daily Telegraph:-

SHEFFIELD GIRL KILLED

WHIRLED ROUND MACHINERY AT VILLAGE FARM

" Employed as a landgirl on a farm at Letwell, a village some six miles from Worksop, Mary (sic) Barlow (24) whose home was in Sheffield, has met a tragic death.

An engine in the machine shed was being prepared for use by the farmer's son who, almost immediately having put on the belting, heard a scream, and saw Miss Barlow being whirled round the shafting.

She fell unconcious as he stopped the engine. Apparently, her head had struck the roof, one of her arms was smashed, and she was dead when Doctor Walliss, Worksop, arrived. It is presumed that the girl had inadvertantly put her hands on the shaft and been drawn up. "

IN LOVING MEMORY OF
JAMES,
THE BELOVED SON OF
JAMES AND AGNES WRIGHT,
ACCIDENTALLY KILLED IN CROW WOOD
JUNE 19th 1914, AGED 4 YEARS.
"JESUS CALLED HIS LITTLE LAMB HOME."

This tragedy was reported in The Sheffield Daily Independent, Saturday, June 20th, 1914:-

TRAGEDY IN A WOOD
BOY PINNED DOWN BY A TREE

"One child was killed and two others were injured yesterday in a terrible accident which befel a party of school children at Intake, Sheffield.
The victim is a boy of four named James Wright, son of a miner living in Main Rd, Intake.
About three o'clock, two teachers and 51 children went to Crow Wood for the purpose of nature study. When they arrived at their favourite clearing in the wood, where several recently felled trees were lying about, most of the children were tired and hot, and at the teacher's direction about 20 of them climbed onto the trunk of a fallen tree which was quite a yard thick at one end and about seven tons in weight.
Hardly had they settled themselves for a rest when a thin sapling that was serving as a wedge slipped out. The huge trunk began to roll down the incline and the babies one and all were carried forward and their legs were dragged underneath.
The child Wright, who was sitting in about the middle of the line was the unfortunate one whose death really saved the lives of all the others for he was dragged so far under that when the tree came to a standstill it was resting heavily straight across his back and neck, and the errant sapling was wedged tightly under his chin. Death was instantaneous, for the poor little chap was frightfully crushed."

Here is another grave which commemorates a man who was killed at work. This edited report is from The Daily Independent dated January 23rd, 1936:-

DEATH WINS AN 18 HOUR FIGHT - MAN TRAPPED IN QUARRY FALL

"A rescue party dug feverishly for 18 hours at a quarry near Frecheville, Sheffield yesterday, in the hope of saving the life of a colleague who had been buried beneath a fall of several tons of clay.
When they managed to release him, they found that their efforts had been in vain, and that he was dead.The man was Samuel Greenfield (36),of 1 Haxton St, Normanton Springs, Sheffield.
The accident occurred shortly after 7.30 on Tuesday night at the quarry and brickyard of Messrs. Fletton Ltd., Birleyvale Brickworks, Intake.
It was not until late yesterday afternoon that the buried man could be released."

IN LOVING MEMORY OF SAMUEL,
BELOVED HUSBAND OF EDITHA GREENFIELD,
WHO WAS ACCIDENTALY (sic)
KILLED AT FLETTONS LTD,
JAN. 21st 1936, AGED 36 YEARS.
SOMETIME WE'LL UNDERSTAND.

CHAPTER FOUR

ART IS THE BEAUTIFUL WAY OF DOING THINGS

"Creative art demands the service of a mind and heart."
William Wordsworth
1770-1850

IT IS refreshing to realise that apart from cutlery workshops, steelworks and all the dirt, smoke and noise which must accompany such things, Sheffield has also produced or nurtured artists and sculptors who rank with the very best in the world.

GODFREY SYKES

Although he was not a Sheffielder, he was born in Malton in 1824, Godfrey Sykes trained for sometime at the School of Art in Arundel Street and later was himself a tutor there. He became skilled in the use of terra cotta as a decorative medium and was later commissioned for design work on the Victoria and Albert Museum in London.

He was also a painter of some note and paintings by him depicting scenes from the work and lives of the inhabitants of Sheffield are owned by the Sheffield Art Galleries. He was commissioned, in 1854, to paint a frieze consisting of a series of separate panels illustrating the arts and crafts of the town, in the lecture theatre of the almost new Mechanics Institute in Surrey Street. This was, for some reason, removed and stored in the cellars of the building during the 1860's. It was rescued in 1930, when the building was demolished and is now in the Sheffield Art Collection.

He died of Bright's Disease, a granular degeneration of the kidneys, aged 41, in London in 1866 and a monument in his memory was erected in Weston Park.

This monument consists of a decorated Corinthian-style column, designed by a pupil, who drew heavily on Sykes' own designs from the Victoria & Albert Museum. The column is in six sections of stone and terra cotta depicting youth, maturity and age alternating with sprays of holly, topped by a Corinthian capital and a bronze vase. The square base is embellished by a bronze plaque of an artists palette and tools and a bronze relief portrait of Sykes, created by Hugh Gamble (1835-1911); the other two sides carry the inscriptions recorded here.

The wording, hyphens and all, is exacly as it is on the memorial:-

GODFREY SYKES BORN
MALTON IN THE
YEAR OF 1824 PUPIL AND
AFTERWARDS MASTER
AT THE SCHOOL OF ART
OF THIS TOWN HE WAS
CALLED TO LONDON IN
THE YEAR 1859 TO SUPER-
-INTEND THE DECORA-
-TION OF THE SOUTH
KENSINGTON MUSEUM
AND DIED THERE 1866.

THIS MONUMENT WAS
ERECTED IN THE YEAR
1871 BY THE INHABIT-
-ANTS OF SHEFFIELD
IN MEMORY OF GODFREY SYKES
THE COLUMN
PLACED UPON THIS
PEDESTAL IS HIS
WORK.

Godfrey Sykes Memorial

Also in Weston Park are what was left, following the theft of the central pair, of a set of lower gates to the park. They were designed by Sykes and assembled and built following Sykes' death. The terra cotta pillars are the same design as the window panels at the Victoria & Albert Museum, where Sykes was working at the time of his death.

A collection of a large amount of his best work can be viewed in The Ceramic Gallery of the Victoria & Albert Museum, London.

SIR FRANCIS CHANTREY RA. FRS.

Francis Legatt Chantrey was born on April 7th, 1781, the son of a small tenant farmer of Norton, which at that time was a small Derbyshire village. He was baptised at the local St. James' Church on May 27th, 1781. As a boy he received the normal education given to a child of his class and, at the age of ten, following his father's death and his mother's remarriage, he was apprenticed until 1804 to Robert Ramsay, a carver and gilder, who worked at 42 High Street, Sheffield.

He was released early from his apprenticeship, by arrangement, when he was 21and in 1802 was in London, where he studied for a time at the Schools of Design, Somerset House, which was part of the Royal Academy. To have been accepted by this "august" establishment without formal qualifications at least, must indicate that his exceptional talent was already apparent. During holidays from his London studies, he returned to Sheffield where he gained both money and useful experience by working as a painter of portraits.

For a short period he rented a small studio in a corner of Paradise Square, where there is a memorial plaque. At this time, he was charging between two and three guineas for his likenesses.

Chantrey Family Grave

He soon realised that his real career lay in the field of sculpture and, in 1806, he produced his first work in marble, a bust of the then Vicar of Sheffield and local magistrate, The Reverend James Wilkinson. This now stands in Sheffield Cathedral.

Prior to that, in 1804, while still in his early twenties, he exhibited for the first time at the Royal Academy. The work was a portrait of Daniel Wale, whose daughter Chantrey married in 1808. His first important commission as a sculptor, and one which did his career no harm at all, was a bust of King George III.

It wasn't until 1810 that he made his permanent base in London, setting up home in Pimlico and it was from there that he entered the most successful period of his life.

He was a prolific producer of sculptures, aided by a large staff which he employed at his workshops, creating likenesses of most of the political, social

Chantrey Memorial

and artistic figures of the time. These included Sir Walter Scott, James Watt, Sir Joseph Banks, plus statues of three English kings, George III, his son, George IV and his brother, William IV. He also produced a life sized statue of Queen Victoria. In his lifetime, he was regarded with great respect by the artistic fraternity and by London society as a whole.

Examples of his work can be seen today in St. Paul's Cathedral, Westminster Abbey and in churches and cathedrals as far apart as Liverpool, Exeter and Norwich. His best known, and perhaps finest piece of sculpture is, "The Sleeping Children", and this is in Lichfield Cathedral, Staffordshire. There are a number of his works to be seen in Sheffield, notably in the Cathedral and the Cutlers Hall.

In 1818, he was elected as a member of both the Royal Society and the Royal Academy and in 1835, he received a knighthood from King William IV. It was said that he later refused a baronetcy.

Chantrey died on November 25th, 1841 and his funeral cortege, drawn by four black horses with four outriders, took six days to return the body to his place of birth. This gives an indication of the level of respect with which he was regarded. He had refused the offer of burial in Westminster Abbey and was buried on December 6th, 1841, at his own request, in the churchyard of his home village of Norton.

A granite memorial 22 feet high, financed by public subscription, was erected on a small green outside the walls of Norton churchyard. It was designed by his friend, Philip Harwick RA, and carries the single word - "CHANTREY"

The family grave, in which his body and those of several of his close relatives are buried, stands to the left of the entrance to St James' Church. It is a simple flat topped tomb protected by wrought iron railings.

M

FRANCIS CHANTREY

DIED MVCCLXVI (1766) AGED LVI (56)

FRANCIS CHANTREY

DIED MVCCXCIII (1793) AGED XXXXV (45)

SARAH HIS WIFE

DIED MVCCCXXVI (1826) AGED LXXXI (81)

This is the inscription of one of the two stones which make up the top of the tomb. This, judging from the dates so inscribed, covers Chantrey's parents and his paternal grandfather. The modern translation of the Roman dates I have added.

On the second stone, covering Chantrey's tomb, the inscription reads:-

SIR FRANCIS CHANTREY

SCULPTOR

RA - FRS

BORN IN THIS PARISH

VII (7) APRIL

MVCCLXXXI (1781)

DIED IN LONDON

NOV XXV (25)

MVCCCXXXXI (1841)

SIR WILLIAM STERNDALE BENNETT

William Bennett was born into a musical family, in a small house at 7 Howard Street. His father was at that time the organist at Sheffield Parish Church, later the cathedral. His life in Sheffield was short as both his parents had died by the time he was four years old and he, together with his sisters, was sent to Cambridge to live with their grandparents.

A precocious boy, he was a member of Kings College Chapel Choir at eight years old and at ten years old he was a student at the Royal Academy of Music. He began composing before he was into his teens and had his first composition performed when he was sixteen years old.

He became a professor of music at Cambridge University when he was forty and ten years later was elected as the Principal of the Royal Academy of Music.

In 1871, he was knighted by Queen Victoria and, four years later, he died in London where he had lived for some time. A public funeral was held and he was buried in Westminster Abbey.

The plaque pictured is in the cathedral in Sheffield which had once employed his father.

CHAPTER FIVE

SHEFFIELD'S SCATTERED SECRETS

"If you would know secrets, look at them in grief or pleasure."
Proverbs

THEY aren't exactly hidden away, but on the other hand neither are they displayed in positions which are prominent enough to be noticed by the people who walk past them everyday. These are the plaques and small memorials which are to be found in little corners tucked away all over the city. There are also many graves in the city's numerous graveyards and cemeteries which, although they do not commemorate particularly famous people, have an edge of interest which is worth noticing.

Sheffield has never been a city which has gone in for the big and elaborate displays that some other places feel are necessary when remembering their distinguished citizens. Not for us the grand gesture. Sir Walter Scott, sitting beneath his grand Victorian creation in Edinburgh, would have fared far more modestly in Sheffield.

There are many people who have plaques in their memory who weren't immensely rich philanthropists, captains of industry or wealthy businessmen, but who still dedicated large portions of their lives to causes that they believed in. In their case, it is possible that since their deaths, without a memorial of some kind, their names could very easily have drifted into obscurity.

This gravestone is in Wardsend Cemetery which ceased to be used for that purpose earlier this century and was abandoned to revert to nature. Many graves, with their ornate and deeply carved stones, have almost disappeared beneath swathes of ground ivy and scrub trees; out of control shrubs and weeds. Recently, however, work by volunteers has begun to return the cemetery to something like its previous condition and it has become once more a pleasant if hilly site to explore.

Notice that the deaths of this married couple occurred within two months of each other:-

ERECTED BY THE
SHEFFIELD ANGLERS
ASSOCIATION
IN AFFECTIONATE REMEMBERANCE OF
THOMAS WALKER,
WHO WAS FOR 29 YEARS SECRETARY
OF THE ABOVE ASSOCIATION,
AND WHO DEPARTED THIS LIFE
AUGUST 6th 1899,
(AT RAMPTON, HIS FAVOURITE
ANGLING RESORT)
AGED 72 YEARS.
ALSO OF MARY ELIZABETH WALKER,
WIFE OF THE ABOVE,
WHO DEPARTED THIS LIFE OCTOBER 2nd, 1899,
AGED 76 YEARS.

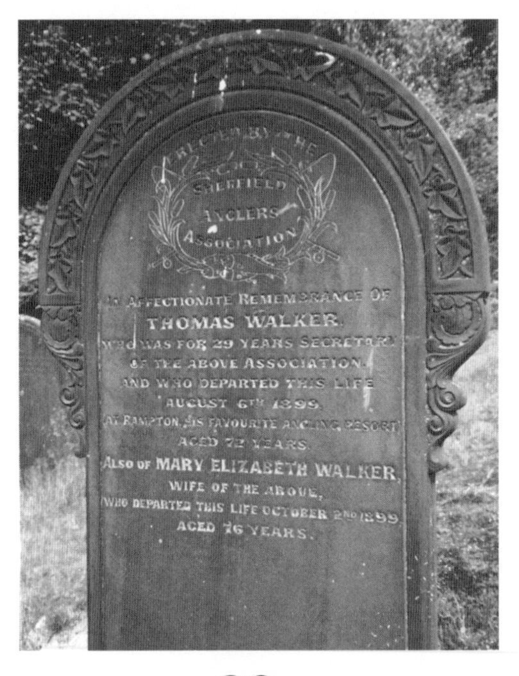

The following two square brass wall plaques are to be found inside the church which stands in the grounds of the now abandoned Middlewood Hospital.

IN MEMORY OF
JAMES ROBERT BARTON
WHO DIED NOVEMBER 25th 1896
FOR 12 YEARS ASSISTANT MEDICAL
OFFICER IN THIS ASYLUM
ERECTED BY HIS COLLEAGUES

IN MEMORY OF
ALICE NEWSOME
ASSISTANT MATRON
WHO DIED SEPTEMBER 16th 1949
AFTER 24 YEARS FAITHFUL SERVICE
IN THESE HOSPITALS
ERECTED BY THE STAFF
MIDDLEWOOD & WHARNCLIFFE HOSPITALS

The following grave is in Burncross Cemetery:-

IN LOVING MEMORY OF
EFFIE MARTIN,
DEAR WIFE OF
WILLIAM HENRY
AWARDED THE FREEDOM OF
ECCLESFIELD PARISH
1973
DIED APRIL 26 1987
AGED 89 YEARS
REUNITED

What this lady did to merit this honour is not known.

St. Mary the Virgin, the parish church of Ecclesfield, was once popularly known as, "The Minster of the Moors." The graveyard that surrounds it contains many graves and tombs of interest.

The section of the graveyard that I am including in this chapter is situated between the wall of the church and the wall separating the graveyard from the gardens of The Priory. It is a shady, narrow area, but here lie some of the most historically important people who have lived in Ecclesfield and its immediate area.

The family tomb of the Gatty family is insignificant. It is fairly small and flat topped.

Dr. Alfred Gatty DD., was the most well known and longest serving of the vicars who have held the living of Ecclesfield. At that time, between 1840 and his death in 1903, he held sway over a far larger parish than is the case today. Ecclesfield, along with many other then villages near Sheffield, was an independent community and the vicar would have been a person of some considerable power and influence over all that happened within his "patch".

The Gatty family were very talented. Dr. Gatty was an historian and writer who added to and updated some of the publications of Joseph Hunter, who is buried nearby and who merits a chapter on his own later in this book. Dr. Gatty's son, Alfred Scott Gatty, was a musician and his wife, Margaret, was also a writer. Her father, Alexander Scott DD., served with Admiral Lord Nelson on board his flagship, HMS Victory, as chaplain and secretary, at the

Battle of Trafalgar, and it is said that he cradled the Admiral in his arms as he lay dying after being shot by a French sniper during the battle. Kiss me, Hardy, and all that!

Probably the most talented writer in the family was the second daughter, Juliana Horatia (note the Nelson influence in her name). She was a well known and respected writer of childrens books. One of her creations, "The Brownies," was the name adopted earlier this century and still used by the junior girls scouting movement.

She was born on August 3rd, 1841 and married an army officer, Major Alexander Ewing, on June 1st, 1867. Her first published work was called, "A Bit of Green", and it appeared in a magazine called, "The Monthly Packet" in July, 1861. Her output was large and it continued until her death aged 43 on May 13th, 1885. She was buried at Trull, near Taunton, Somerset, where her husband was serving at the time.

HERE LIE BURIED
ALEXANDER JOHN SCOTT DD,
VICAR OF CATTERICK AND SOUTHMINSTER
AND CHAPLAIN TO ADMIRAL LORD NELSON
ON BOARD HMS VICTORY AT TRAFALGAR
HE DIED JULY 24 1840 AGED 72
ALSO HIS DAUGHTER
MARGARET
THE BELOVED WIFE OF ALFRED GATTY DD
VICAR OF ECCLESFIELD
SHE DIED OCTOBER 4 1873 AGED 64
ALSO HER INFANT SONS
ALFRED ALEXANDER GATTY
WHO DIED MARCH 22 1844 AND
HORATIO NELSON GATTY
WHO DIED OCTOBER 2 1855
HERE ALSO RESTS THE BODY OF
ALFRED GATTY DD
BORN 18 APRIL 1813
DIED 20 JANUARY 1903
VICAR OF ECCLESFIELD FOR 63 YEARS
AND SUB DEAN OF YORK

The tomb of the Ryder family, slightly larger, but also flat topped, is adjacent to the Gatty tomb.

Thomas Ryder was vicar of Ecclesfield just before Dr. Gatty. He died on July 24th, 1839, aged 44 years old. Buried with him in the grave are his wife, Anne, and their four daughters. Also commemorated is his youngest son, Thomas Ryder, who was a lieutenant in Her Majesty's 3rd Bombay European Regiment. He died on February 8th, 1861, in his 32nd year and was buried in Richmond, Yorkshire. If he is buried in England, then as his regiment served almost exclusively in India, he either died while home on leave or his body was brought back. The latter seems unlikely.

The third important family grave in this part of the churchyard is, at first sight, not particularly impressive, but it represents a wealth of history concerning one of the most well known of the local families.

The Smith family, now fairly well dispersed, were the owners of Barnes Hall, a moderately large house with attendant farming land and buildings, which still stands today in the area just outside Ecclesfield known as Bracken Hill. It first came into the family in 1823.

The patriach of the part of the Smith family commemorated in this plot was Francis Patrick Smith, who had nine sons. He was born in 1835 and married the daughter of Dr Alfred Gatty DD, Margaret Scott Gatty. This links the Smith family with the previously described Gatty family. Francis was the third son of William Smith, who inherited Barnes Hall from his father, also named William.

The first William, Francis Smith's grandfather, who died in 1849, had replaced the hall in 1823, having first demolished the original buildings on the site. He had bought the estate earlier the same year and it then consisted of the hall, farm buildings, five almshouses and about 120 acres of farmland.

In 1829, William helped to form the Ecclesfield Association for the Prosecution of Felons. There were 84 signatories to this association when it was first set up and its objective was to fund the prosecution of anyone committing a felony against them or their property. This was considered necessary because the local law enforcer, the constable, which was an unpaid, yearly appointed job, was proving inefficient. These were, of course, men who had sufficient property and wealth to worry about such things!

Francis Smith's father, William, married Mary Anne Mackenzie, the daughter of the Rev. Alexander Mackenzie, the vicar of St. Paul's Church, Sheffield. This large and important church was built between 1720 and 1740 and was demolished earlier this century by the council, with the intention of using the site to build a town hall extension. These plans were abandoned when the Second World War broke out and the site became The Peace Gardens.

William and Mary had 13 children who were supported by his activities both as a farmer and as a solicitor. Later in life, in partnership with his neighbour and friend, Mr Jeffcock, he opened a bank on Bank Street, Sheffield which stood until destroyed by enemy action during the 1940's.

William was a typical country squire and fond of vintage port which may have helped him to live to the venerable age of 93 years.

Upon his father's death, Francis Patrick Smith inherited Barnes Hall in 1888, where he followed his father in combining the law with farming.

Several of his nine sons served in the army - in the Boer War and in the First World War. Two of them, the eldest, William, and his brother, Leonard, both became colonels and each were awarded the DSO. A third brother, George, became a major.

When Francis died, he was succeeded by his eldest son, also William, known locally as "The Colonel". He married Lady Mabel, the sister of the 7th Earl Fitzwilliam of Wentworth Woodhouse. He worked with his nephew, Sydney, the son of his brother Godfrey, who at the time was Archdeacon of Barrow in Furness, at the family law firm of Smith, Smith & Fielding. This firm amalgamated with another local law firm, Wake & Sons, to become Wake Smith. This firm is still practicing today.

Lady Mabel was childless, but led a busy and fruitful life. She was first a member and then an alderman of the old West Riding County Council. She was also a stalwart of the Workers Education Association and was involved in social welfare work with a special interest in all aspects of workers' education. When her family home, Wentworth Woodhouse, became a training college for women teachers, it was named Lady Mabel College as a tribute to her tireless work.

Both "The Colonel" and his Lady lived into their 80's and when they died were buried beneath the shade of the lime trees in Ecclesfield's lovely little churchyard.

There are three gravestones marking this family plot and although the inscriptions are lengthy I felt that it would be a pity to edit them:-

The right hand stone:-

IN MEMORY OF
FRANCIS PATRICK SMITH
OF BARNES HALL, ECCLESFIELD,
WHO DIED AUGUST 30th 1919
AGED 84 YEARS
AND OF HIS THIRD SON
STEPHEN ALEXANDER
WHO DIED 23rd DECEMBER 1927
AGED 55 YEARS
AND OF HIS FIFTH SON
LEONARD KIRKE, CBE, DSO,
COLONEL, ROYAL SCOTS
WHO DIED 23rd MARCH 1941
AGED 64 YEARS
AND OF HIS NINTH SON
GEORGE MACKENZIE
MAJOR, EAST LANCASHIRE REGT
WHO DIED 26th DECEMBER 1941
AGED 58

The rear of the right hand stone:-

IN MEMORY
OF
VERA
WIFE OF
LEONARD KIRKE SMITH
WHO DIED SEPt 6th 1973,
AGED 82 YEARS.

The left hand stone:-

IN MEMORY OF
MARGARET SCOTT
THE BELOVED WIFE OF
FRANCIS PATRICK SMITH
OF BARNES HALL, SHEFFIELD
WHO DIED SEPTEMBER 16th 1900
AGED 60 YEARS
AND OF
MABEL FLORENCE HARRIET
WIFE OF
WILLIAM MACKENZIE SMITH
WHO DIED SEPTEMBER 26th 1951
AGED 81 YEARS
AND OF THE ABOVE
WILLIAM MACKENZIE SMITH
DSO, TD, LLD
COLONEL, QUEENS OWN YORKSHIRE
DRAGOONS
ELDEST SON OF FRANCIS PATRICK SMITH
DIED AUGUST 16th 1956
AGED 87 YEARS.

The rear of the left hand stone:-

IN MEMORY OF
GILBERT KIRKE SMITH
EIGHTH SON OF
FRANCIS PATRICK SMITH
WHO DIED DECEMBER 3rd
1967
AGED 86 YEARS
AND OF HIS WIFE
MARGERY
WHO DIED MARCH 5th 1970
AGED 81 YEARS

The third stone:-

HERE RESTS
THE BODY OF
MARGARET,
SECOND DAUGHTER OF JOSEPH CASTLING,
SCHOOLMASTER, OF BOLTON-ON-SWALE,
FOR 30 YEARS NURSE AND FRIEND
IN THE FAMILY OF F.P. SMITH,
OF BARNES HALL, WHERE SHE DIED
AUGUST 18th 1899, AGED 47 YEARS.
THEM THAT SLEEP IN JESUS
WILL GOD BRING WITH HIM.
ALSO OF SARAH. M. GUY,
WHO DIED AT BARNES HALL,
5th MAY 1927, AGED 84 YEARS,
THE LIFELONG FRIEND OF MABEL SMITH.

It is rather surprising that a family which at one time was so well known, so numerous in its offspring and holding such an importance position in the neighbourhood can lose its influence in an area so quickly.

Outside the wall of the large house, Norton Hall, which abuts Norton church, there is an engraved drinking trough, now used for flowers. This is one of the local memorials to Annie Hall, wife of a vicar of Norton. It is engraved:-

TO THE
MEMORY OF
ANNIE HALL
OF NORTON VICARAGE
ERECTED BY
PARISHIONERS AND
OTHER FRIENDS
A.D. 1905

In the actual churchyard there is another memorial to her in the form of a celtic cross, heavily engraved:-

IN CHERISHED MEMORY OF
ANNIE
THE VERY LOVED AND REVERED WIFE OF
GEORGE WALKER HALL,
VICAR OF THIS PARICH,
BORN APRIL 21st 1840,
DIED JANUARY 27th 1904.
SHE LIVED TO MAKE OTHERS HAPPY THOUGH
LONG AFFLICTED, HER LIFE WAS FULL OF
ACTIVE SERVICE BRIGHT WITH THE BEAMS OF
HEAVENLY LOVE WHICH SHED ITS GRACIOUS
SMILE UPON ALL AROUND HER.
ALSO
THE ABOVE GEORGE WALKER HALL.

Mrs Hall has several other memorials inside the main body of the church - a window, a mural tablet and the figures of martyrs added to the pulpit surrounds. The lady must have been well respected and much missed to have gathered such a rich crop of memorabilia.

Inside Norton churchyard, propped up against the wall with several others is a very old and rather crudely executed tombstone reading:-

HERE LYETH Ye BODY
OF JONATHAN BOOTH
DYED JAN'Y Ye 18
1762 AGED 44

Jonathan Booth was, I believe, a small farmer of Norton Woodseats. His wife, Elizabeth, whose maiden name was Wood, was the daughter of Stephen and Isabella Wood of Summerley, near Dronfield. Elizabeth was a devoutly religious woman, although this initially caused domestic problems. A quotation taken from "Chantrey Land" by Harold Armitage, reads:- " The opposition which she first had from her husband, who, through the persuasion of his relatives, threatened to turn her out of doors, was considerable. Though she brought him a fortune (presumably as a dowry), he would not, on the testimony of a daughter, suffer to have a halfpenny in her possession to his knowledge, and she frequently contributed to her class by the saving of a farthing at a time. She generally attended preaching at Sheffield at five o'clock in the morning, carrying the child in her arms that she was then nursing. Through her perseverance and exemplary conduct she at length so won upon him, as to suffer preaching to be established in the house; and through some severe affliction in the family, he was thus brought to serious reflection, and lived in fear and love of God for several years."

Elizabeth was born in 1725 and later became interested in Methodism. John Wesley, one of the founders of this to some extent outlawed religion, often preached in Woodseats and was a visitor, along with other early Methodist preachers, to the Booths' house.

Another tombstone, also against a wall, is interesting because it shows another example of a presumably long married couple who died within a very short time of each other - in this case a matter of a few days:-

IN MEMORY OF
ROBERT BOOKER
OF LEES HALL
WHO DIED SEPTEMBER 27th 1863 AGED 83 YEARS
ALSO OF ELLEN-HIS WIFE
WHO DIED SEPTEMBER 21st 1863
AGED 76 YEARS

The Blythe (or Blyth) family have deep roots in Norton and the surrounding area. The William Blythe described on the gravestone below was an officer in the Parliamentary Army during the Civil War. In 1646, the House of Commons, which was dominated by the parliamentarians, decided that the castle at Sheffield should be rendered undefendable and a year later ordered that it should be destroyed completely. It was William Blythe who was empowered to order this work and it was his hand which signed the demolition order. Thus, Sheffield lost its castle. Upon the reinstatement of the monarchy, he was given a free pardon for his actions by Charles II.

He died in 1665 and his gravestone, which was once inside the main body of the church, is today set into the wall of the church porch. It is in fair condition, considering its age, although the bottom half has been recut.

HERE LIETH
THE BODYE OF
WILLIAM BLYTHE
OF NORTON LEESE
WHO WAS BVRIED
THE 9th OF FEBRVARY
IN THE YEAR 1665
BEING THE 57th (YEAR) OF HIS AGE

Another gravestone set into the wall of the porch was removed from inside the church when it was refurbished in 1882. It commemorates a woman who was buried standing up for some reason. Her name was Barbara Lee and she died in October 1670, aged 28 years. The inscription on the stone is in Latin and in poor condition.

In Tinsley Park Cemetery there is a grave which is unusual in that it is in memory of two brothers who both died aged 22 years old, but years and many thousands of miles apart.

IN LOVING MEMORY
OF
ROBERT, SON OF
GEORGE &
FLORENCE
INKERSOLE
KILLED IN CANADA
OCT 29th 1924
AGED 22 YEARS
ALSO OF
THOMAS ARTHUR
BROTHER OF THE
ABOVE
DIED JULY 1st 1932
AGED 22 YEARS

This family grave of the Jacobs' is in Shiregreen Cemetery and carries a similar unusual inscription. From the dates, it seems possible that both young men might have been servicemen, but there is no indication of this on the gravestone.

TO THE MEMORY OF
OUR BELOVED SONS
HAROLD
DIED 17th NOV. 1942 AGED 24 YEARS.
AND ARNOLD
DIED 19th OCT. 1944 AGED 24 YEARS.

This grave commemorates the premature death of the son of one of Sheffield's leading Jewish families. It is in the small Jewish section of Walkley Cemetery, which was opened in 1872 and dedicated by the Chief Rabbi, Nathan Adler.

Marcus was the eldest son of Harris Leon Brown, better known as HL Brown, a name which is well known in the city for the upmarket jewellery and watchmakers shop in the centre of Sheffield.

He was born in Warsaw in 1843, son of Baruch Braun, who was a Russian government contractor. He became an apprentice to the large Warsaw company of Moses Neufeld, who imported many products which were Sheffield made.

Following an insurrection against Russian despotism, HL Braun left Poland and settled in Sheffield. He had introductions to the firms of Messrs. Alfred Beckett & Sons and Messrs. Berry & Co. These firms helped him to settle in Sheffield and through their help he found both employment and a home. Beginning in the jewellery business by selling watches to his workmates, he also joined the Hallamshire Rifles as a token of his gratitude for his acceptance in Sheffield.

His business flourished, and in time there were branches in several towns; he also became jeweller to the Duke of Norfolk and watchmaker to the Admiralty. He died in 1917.

This grave has a large, slightly askew, brown marble obelisk; the top part of the inscription is in Hebrew, the bottom part in English.

IN LOVING MEMORY OF
MARCUS, ELDEST SON OF H.L.BROWN
WHO DIED APRIL 13th 1887.
AGED 17 YEARS AND 10 MONTHS.

(Above the name HL Brown on the stone is the name, in small letters, Hannah. This must have been his mother and was added later.)

The following obituary notice is taken from The Sheffield Daily Telegraph, dated 16th April, 1887:-

"BROWN - April 13, after a long and painful illness,
at the residence of his parents, Warsaw House,
Sharrow, Sheffield, Marcus Brown, the dearly beloved
son of H.L. Brown, aged 18. Friends will please
accept this intimation."

In Tinsley Park Cemetery, there is an unusual monument set into a stone wall almost at the top of the cemetery. It is rather gruesome, if you think too much about its wording.

THIS PLAQUE WAS PRESENTED BY
THE UNIVERSITY OF SHEFFIELD
IN GRATEFUL MEMORY
OF ALL THOSE BURIED HERE
WHO LEFT THEIR BODIES
FOR THE FURTHERANCE OF
MEDICAL TEACHING

I don't want to dwell on this plaque for long, but just to wonder what was buried, in what sort of a grave and where?

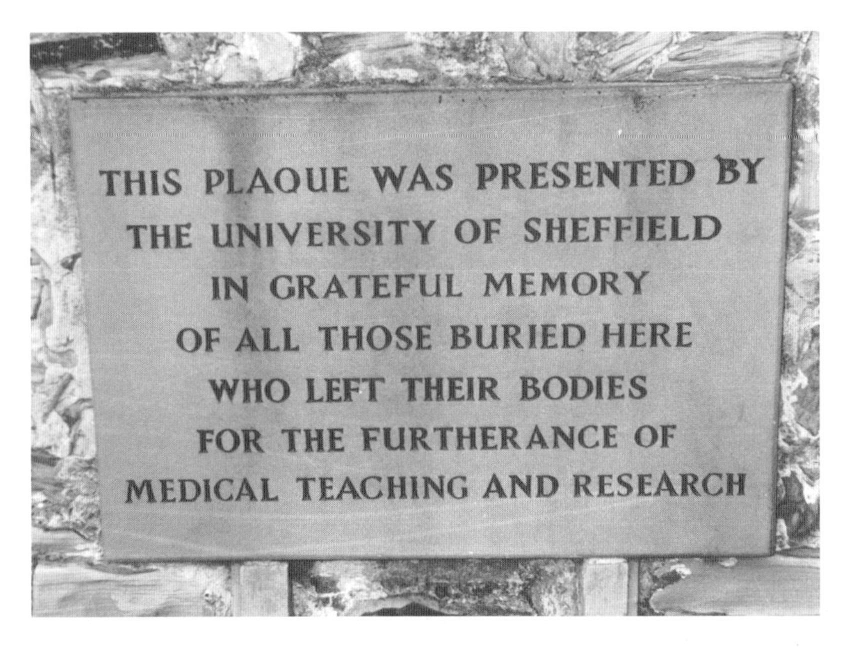

Here are four graves from the crowded little churchyard at Dore. The first plot has two identical family graves surrounded by a chain. The graves have various family inscriptions on them. These below are the most interesting ones:-

IN MEMORY OF
CHARLES EDWARD WATERFALL
LATE OF HMS "ARROGANT"
SON OF JOHN GRAY WATERFALL AND ANN HIS
WIFE WHO DIED AUGUST THE 7th 1852
IN THE 19th YEAR OF HIS AGE.
ALSO OF THEIR SON JOHN HENRY WATERFALL
LATE OF HM 5th ROYAL LANCERS AND
PREVIOUSLY OF HM 95th REGIMENT
WHO DIED DECEMBER THE 1st 1863
IN THE 31st YEAR OF HIS AGE.

This grave has a small mystery attached to it. Why should the Town Clerk of Wigan be buried in Sheffield?

IN LOVING
MEMORY
OF
JOHN JAMES
CHARNOCK,
SOLICITOR AND
TOWN CLERK
OF WIGAN, FROM
1895 TO 1900
WHO DIED OCTr
13th 1900
AGED 47 YEARS.

This grave has one of those wonderful, highly descriptive and fulsome Victorian descriptions on it. Was this because he was a man who contributed "materially" to the upkeep of the church?

IN MEMORY OF
THOMAS BIGGIN, OF DORE FIELDS,
WHO DIED APRIL 11th 1861,
AGED 27 YEARS.
REGRETTED BY ALL FOR THE KINDLINESS OF HIS DISPOSITION. A GOOD MASTER AMONG HIS MEN, A GOOD FRIEND AMONG HIS EQUALS.
HE WAS A WARM SUPPORTER OF ALL PAROCHIAL INSTITUTIONS, AND CONTRIBUTED MATERIALLY TO THE RECENT IMPROVEMENTS IN THE CHURCH AND SCHOOLS.

This final gravestone from Dore Churchyard also eulogizes one of its occupants:-

IN MEMORY OF
THOMAS BOOKER,
WHO FOR TWENTY ONE YEARS OCCUPIED
THE CROFT HOUSE FARM IN DORE,
DISTINGUISHED AMONG HIS FRIENDS AND
EQUALS BY THE SIMPLICITY OF HIS MANNERS,
AND UNVARYING HONESTY OF PURPOSE, HE
PASSED WITH THE RESPECT OF ALL, IN PEACE
AND CONTENTMENT THROUGH HIS LIFE,
AND DIED IN FAITHFUL HOPE
OF A BETTER ONE
SEPTEMBER 1st 1862, AGED 61 YEARS.
ALSO ELIZABETH, WIFE OF THE ABOVE
WHO DIED NOVEMBER 18th 1882,
AGED 73 YEARS.

In Hillsborough Park, in the memorial garden behind the house, there are two memorial stones. They don't belong there, but this is where they have finished up and here they will probably remain. The garden is beside the walled garden and commemorates those lives which were lost at Hillsborough Stadium during a football match in 1989.

This first stone is a long, narrow slab of slate, about one foot wide and five feet long. It appears to have once been mounted on a wall.

SACRED TO THE MEMORY OF
ELIZA, THE BELOVED WIFE OF HENRY
ELLIOTT HOOLE, OF SHEFFIELD, MERCHANT,
AND DAUGHTER OF THE LATE JOHN WALLIS
ESQr. FORMERLY OF PORTSLADE, BRIGHTON:
SHE DIED ON THE 5th FEBRUARY, 1836, IN THE
24th YEAR OF HER AGE.
ALSO OF HENRY WALLIS HOOLE, THEIR ONLY
CHILD, WHO DIED FROM THE EFFECTS OF AN
ACCIDENTAL FALL ON THE 20th AUGUST 1847,
AT HUTHWAITE HALL IN THIS
NEIGHBOURHOOD,
IN THE 12th YEAR OF HIS AGE.
"IN THE MIDST OF LIFE WE ARE IN DEATH."

The second stone appears to have been designed to lie flat on the ground to cover a grave. It is about eighteen inches wide by four feet long and rises to a ridge in the centre. The words at the end of the inscription seem to indicate that there was some sort of trouble in Wardsend Cemetery in 1862.

TO THE AFFECTIONATE REMEMBERANCE
OF FRANK BACON,
WHO DEPARTED THIS LIFE APRIL 2nd 1854,
AGED THREE YEARS.
ALSO LOUIS BACON, AGED 4 MONTHS.
BURIED IN WARDSEND CEMETERY
APRIL 12th 1853,
AND WAS ONE OF THE MANY FOUND IN 1862,
WHO HAD BEEN SO RUTHLESSLY
DISENTERRED.

The last line of this inscription poses a puzzle. Was this the work of the so called "resurrectionists"? These were the goulish creatures whose grisly trade was to dig up freshly buried corpses and sell them to the local medical schools for dissection purposes. This practice was known as "burking", after Burke and Hare, the famous Edinburgh body snatchers.

I don't really think so, as the baby's body had been in the ground for nine years before it was disturbed.

CHAPTER SIX

THE MAKERS OF SHEFFIELD

"If you have genius, industry will improve it;
If you have none, industry will supply its place."

Sir Joshua Reynolds
1723-1792

ALTHOUGH intense international competition and the use of mass production methods has today undermined greatly the reputation and the number of companies still involved in the cutlery trade, it was this business and also the huge steelworks, mostly now also defunct, which were the bedrock on which the reputation of Sheffield was built.

Many of the men who began the great steel and cutlery businesses which dominated the city for so long, were self-made men who rose from relatively poor backgrounds and who, through sheer hard work and probably a good measure of Yorkshire grit and bloody mindedness, created names which became well known worldwide.

A large number of these great men, and unfortunately they are all men, have nothing much by way of memorials to celebrate their lives, apart from their gravestones, and in some cases even these have almost disappeared. To some of them, perhaps, this is how they would have preferred it. After all, if you create, control and then leave behind a huge steelworks or cutlery business which bears your name, there isn't really much else needed is there? Or an art gallery, which came into being through your generosity; or a technical college, which your money built?

The great men of Sheffield have done all of these things, as well as building churches and donating land for parks and gardens. The Jessop Hospital bears the name of Thomas Jessop, the steel manufacturer, which was opened in 1878 and which cost him about £30,000. Mark Firth, also a steelman, endowed the Firth College, which opened a year later on the corner of West Street and Leopold Street. There are many other examples. The list is long and a credit to these men.

This folio contains only a few names; there will be others to follow in future volumes.

THOMAS BOULSOVER

In the manner of many other discoveries which have led to the introduction of todays common processes, the method by which Old Sheffield Plate came into being was an accident. In about 1742, while working as a cutler, Thomas Boulsover was repairing a knife handle which was made in parts of copper and of silver. By mistake he overheated the metals and the two components fused together. Thinking, no doubt, about the damage and what he was going to do to rectify it, he realised then that it was possible, given the right conditions, to cover clean copper with a thin layer of silver and that the resulting product could be used to make articles which would have the appearance of silver, but which could be produced at a fraction of the cost. Thus, Old Sheffield Plate was born.

Boulsover was, by all accounts, not a very ambitious businessman and he left the exploitation and subsequent profit from his discovery to others. He preferred to concentrate on the production of small, mundane articles such as silver buttons, shoe buckles and the like, while others took up the process and made tea services, trays and all manner of large and profitable products.

He took Joseph Wilson on as a partner and built a rolling mill and forge on the River Porter at Whiteley Woods and in the course of this business he became sufficiently prosperous to be able to buy the nearby Whiteley Wood Hall. It was there that he died on December 12th, 1788. He was buried in the churchyard of the now demolished St Paul's Church which used to stand on the Peace Gardens site.

When the area now known as Tudor Square was developed in 1991, a bronze relief of Thomas Boulsover standing on a granite base was unveiled and the inscription on the monument reads:-

THOMAS
BOULSOVER
1705 - 1788
INVENTOR OF
OLD SHEFFIELD PLATE
THOMAS BOULSOVER MADE THE
CHANCE DISCOVERY OF
THE FUSION OF COPPER AND
SILVER ON THIS SITE IN 1743.
THIS INVENTION CREATED A
THRIVING INDUSTRY AND
HELPED SHEFFIELD TO PROSPER.

Although the inscription states "on this site", I'm not sure that there is any historical evidence to back up this statement.

WILLIAM BUTCHER

The son of James Butcher, a cutler of Charles Street, who died in 1806 aged 45, William was born about 1791. He was followed by his brother and future business partner, Samuel, six years later.

The brothers probably learned the cutlery trade in the usual fashion before going into business for themselves. In 1819, they rented some premises in Eyre Lane and began producing edge tools, saws, files and similar and in 1822, they began to produce their own crucible steel.

They were initially a small firm, one among many others, but they saw an opening in North America, worked to develop it and in the 1830's they expanded into the lucrative American market. It proved to be a successful business venture and by the 1840's the firm had expanded into additional manufacturing and forging space in the Philadelphia Works.

All this expansion of the firm was needed in the 1850's and 1860's when Sheffield's trade with the USA increased manyfold. The Butchers' were extremely successful in the Bowie knife market in addition to a wide range of tools such as files, trowels and chisels.

By the end of this fruitful business era, the Butcher Brother's Company employed about 1,000 craftsmen and it was reported that they were producing, from their own steel, 12 tons of files, 600 dozen chisels, 400 dozen planes and 800 dozen razors a week. This was from the Philadelphia Works alone. If true, and there is no reason to doubt the accuracy of the figures, this was an amazing output.

Shortly after Willam Butcher retired, he lost his second wife, Elizabeth, who died in 1867; his brother, Samuel, died in 1869, aged 73 years old, at his home in Banner Cross, (the inscription on his tomb is very badly eroded and impossible to read accurately) and William himself died, aged 79, at his home, Five Oaks, in Glossop Road, on November 8th, 1870. Of his family he was survived by only two daughters.

The tombstone inscription reads:-

TO THE GLORY
OF GOD
AND IN MEMORY OF
WILLIAM
BUTCHER
OF FIVE OAKS
SHEFFIELD
WHO ENTERED
INTO REST
NOVEMBER
8th 1870 IN
THE 79th YEAR
OF HIS AGE

Willam Butcher left about £100,000 and is buried in All Saints Parish Churchyard, Ecclesall, close to his brother, beneath a high, marble, celtic cross now ivy covered and almost forgotten. Inside the church, there is a memorial on the wall to his two wives and his children.

Also commemorated on the grave are his first wife, Eliza, born 8th February, 1796, died 23rd May, 1833; his second wife, Elizabeth, born 7th September, 1790, died 29th December, 1867; his two sons, James Thomas and William and his daughter, Ann.

SIR JOHN BROWN JP. DL.

John Brown was born in Favell's Yard, off Fargate, on December 6th, 1816. He was the second son of Samuel Brown, a relatively comfortably off builder and roofer and his wife, Anne. When he died, eighty years later, hundreds of miles away in Bromley, Kent, he had left a lasting mark on his native city and a name which survives today. He had invented one of the basic things which is still used on railways all over the world, built up one of the largest steel and armament businesses the country has ever seen and made, and to a large extent lost, a fortune.

Following a simple education at the local "Dame" school, he was apprenticed to the firm of Earl, Horton & Co, who were general traders, later to become makers of files and cutlery, situated in Rockingham Street. He progressed well and when he reached 21, he was offered and accepted a partnership in the firm. This was financed by £500 raised, possibly not without some difficulty, by his father and an uncle.

His role in the company was as a salesman and he travelled the north of England in a pony and trap which was loaded with the company's wares. This continued until he set up in business for himself in 1844 as a steelmaker. He was perceptive enough to recognise that there was money to be made from the ever increasing mileage of railway lines which, during the middle of the 19th Century, were spreading across the countryside and he concentrated on making these as well as assorted accessories for railway rolling stock.

In 1848, he invented what was to prove in later years to be a foundation stone of his business empire - the conical steel spring railway buffer. This invention was eventually used on almost all the railway systems in the country. Brown realised its importance in his fortunes and later in life he incorporated it into the design of his coat of arms.

As business increased and the company prospered, so did the number of industrial sites. Seizing a bargain, Brown bought the former Queen's Works on Savile Street at a knock down price from a firm which was verging on the edge of bankruptcy. He renamed it Atlas Works and, from January 1st, 1856, all his production was centralised on the three acre site. Within a few years the whole site was prospering and there was more success to come.

In 1859, Brown entered into partnership with two men from Birmingham, John D Ellis and William Bragge, to form the John Brown Company. In 1861, the company began employing the recently invented Bessamer steel process and after suffering a few of the teething troubles which often accompany a new process, by 1865 the company was producing half the railway lines being laid in Britain.

Armour plate manufacturing followed and by 1867, John Brown Co. were supplying the Royal Navy with three quarters of the armour plate needed to protect its ships. It must not be forgotten that at this stage in world history, Britain had a navy larger than the combined navies of any other two countries!

Soon Brown and his company were one of the largest employers in Sheffield. In 1857, he needed about 200 employees, but by 1867, this number had increased to 4,000; the company had an annual turnover in excess of £1 million and the original three acre site had swelled to over twenty acres, all in full use.

The Tomb of Sir John Brown

This was John Brown at the pinnacle of his business career. After that, the business, his personal fortunes and his health went into decline. The slump in business was in tune with the reduction in demand for his company's armour plate. Brown did not stay with the slowly sinking ship, but in 1871 sold out his shares and left the company intent on pursuing his many other interests. This he did with mixed financial results.

By the 1880's, following the death of his wife, Mary, whom he had married in 1839, and plagued by recurring bouts of ill health, Brown retired from active business life. In 1892, he left Sheffield to live in the south of England, selling his magnificent suburban mansion, Endcliffe Hall, which had cost him about £150,000 to build, for what was believed to have been a mere fraction of its true worth. Today it still stands and is military property.

Plaque in Orchard Square near the site of Favell's Yard

John Brown gives the impression that, at this stage of life, with no wife to support him and share his life, no businesses to sustain him and often ill, he was an unhappy and, in some ways, a disappointed man.

During what was in the end a long life, John Brown was the recipient of numerous honours. He was knighted by Queen Victoria in 1867, one of the few great Sheffield men to receive this honour; he was Master Cutler in both 1865 and 1866; Mayor in 1862-63 and was then created an alderman of the town. In 1864, he was appointed a town trustee and was chief magistrate from 1862.

A staunch member of the Church of England, he still found the time and compassion to help needy people of all or no religious denominations. There is no statue in the city to John Brown, so perhaps his most famous memorial is All Saints Church, which was first consecrated in 1869.

When he died on 27th December, 1896, his body was returned to Sheffield and interred in the graveyard of All Saints Parish Church, Ecclesall, next to his wife, Mary. Financially, he left the rather unexpectedly small sum of £27,221, but as one of the great pioneering, self-made steelmen, his name will always be remembered in Sheffield.

The inscription on Sir John Brown's tomb reads:-

SACRED
TO THE MEMORY OF
SIR JOHN BROWN, J.P. D.L.
OF ENDCLIFFE HALL,
SHEFFIELD.
WHO DIED DECr 27th 1896,
AGED 80 YEARS.
ALSO OF
MARY, HIS BELOVED WIFE
WHO DIED NOVr 28th 1881,
AGED 68 YEARS.

There is another memorial to Sir John Brown and this is in Orchard Square. It is an oval, brass or bronze plaque and is fixed to a brick pillar adjacent to Waterstone's Bookshop. The inscription reads:-

THE CITY OF SHEFFIELD

JOHN BROWN

JOHN BROWN (1816 - 1896),

ONE OF THE GREATEST OF THE VICTORIAN
INDUSTRIALISTS, WAS BORN IN ORCHARD
SQUARE, IN WHAT WAS THEN FAVELL'S YARD.
HE WAS APPRENTICED IN NEARBY ORCHARD
PLACE BEFORE SETTING UP HIS FIRST
STEELMAKING WORKSHOP IN 1844 AT NUMBER
24 ORCHARD STREET. INVENTOR OF THE
CONICAL SPRING RAILWAY BUFFER AND
PIONEER MANUFACTURER OF RAILWAY LINES
AND ARMOUR PLATE, HIS NAME LIVED ON
INTO THE TWENTIETH CENTURY THROUGH
THE STEEL FORGINGS PRODUCED AT FIRTH
BROWN FOR THE FAMOUS BATTLESHIPS AND
LINERS BUILT AT THE JOHN BROWN
SHIPYARDS, CLYDEBANK.

HENRY BOOT

The building firm founded by Henry Boot is still flourishing today in Sheffield. Henry Boot was born in 1851, the son of a small farmer in the Heeley area of Sheffield, which at that time was more countryside than town. He started his working life with a seven year long joinery apprenticeship and followed it with many years of working at the practicalities of the building trade before, at the age of 35, buying a horse and cart and starting out in business for himself.

When he died in 1931, aged 80 years old, he left behind a family building firm, which is still in the hands of his descendants and which now has worldwide connections.

Like many companies at the time, Henry Boot & Sons, found opportunities for advancement during the years of the First World War and in that period they built many military buildings and laid miles of roads and sewers. After the war, the company spread to France and was employed rebuilding the war damaged villages and towns in the battle areas.

Between the wars, the company expanded even more and claims to have built 80,000 houses during that period, many more than any other single company.

Today, the company takes on contracts as far apart as Nigeria and Malaysia and although its head office is still in Ecclesall Road, Sheffield, it has a presence in most major European cities.

When Henry Boot died, he was buried in Crookes Cemetery, along with his wife who died in 1941 and three daughters, Ruth Mace, died in 1942; Gertrude Helen, died in 1935 and Edith Anne, died in 1975.

CHAPTER SEVEN

ABOVE AND BEYOND THE CALL OF DUTY

"True valour lies between cowardice and rashness."

Saavedra Miguel de Cervantes

1547-1616

HERE are few men indeed alive today who are entitled to wear the small and almost insignificant cross with its crimson ribbon which is the Victoria Cross.

The British have always made a virtue out of understatement and, in this medal, the highest award for bravery in the face of the enemy that the nation can bestow, the award which takes precedence over any other decoration of any kind, they have excelled themselves.

It is officially described as, "a cross-pattee of bronze, one and a half inches in diameter, with the Royal Crown surmounted by a lion in the centre, beneath which there is the inscription, For Valour". Since its introduction by Queen Victoria on 29th January, 1856, about 2,000 VC's have been awarded, most of whom are now dead.

In 1980, there were 96 men still surviving who were winners of this award; by 1991, this number had shrunk to 46 and in 1995, the last figures that I have been able to locate, the survivors were down to only 33. Of these men, 30 had won their medal in the last war, one had been won in 1951 during the Korean War, one in Sarawak in 1965 and one in the Vietnam War in 1969.

The last two men to have won the VC both died in action - Col. H Jones and Sgt. McKay. This was during the Falklands War.

Sheffield, as far as I can discover, has connections with six VC winners, although only three of these men were actually born in the town - Arnold Loosemore, William Barnsley Allen and John Crawshaw Raynes. The other three men were George Lambert, born in County Antrim, Northern Ireland; Rev. Arthur Herbert Proctor, born in Bootle, Lancashire and James Firth, believed to have been born in Jarrow, County Durham.

Two of the men, whose actions are described below are buried in Sheffield; the third man has a memorial tablet in the cathedral.

Sgt. ARNOLD LOOSEMORE V.C., D.C.M.

This is an account taken from the London Gazette, 14th September, 1917:-

"Arnold Loosemore was born in Sharrow, Sheffield in the year 1897, the son of Joseph and Mary Loosemore. He was the youngest of seven brothers, who all attended Clifford Road Church of England School. At the outbreak of war in 1914, all his brothers were of age to join up and he tried at the Recruiting Depot, but was turned away as being too young. At the time he was working as a farmer's boy at Fulwood, but he left to work for a coal merchant to try and build up his physique to be accepted by the Army. Eventually, he made it at the age of seventeen, giving a false age, as did so many in those days.

He was drafted into the York & Lancaster Regiment and served with them in the Dardanelles. On returning to England, he was transferred to the 14th Duke of Wellington's Regiment and sent out to France.

At one time before going up the line they were in camp and he was cleaning his Lewis gun when two aircraft appeared. When he realised that the front one was being followed by a German plane, he fired at the rear one and brought it down. Later in the day, an Air Force staff car visited their camp and it was the pilot of the front plane who had come to thank the gunner who had saved his life. For this deed he was promoted to corporal.

Sgt. Loosemore's Grave in Ecclesall Cemetery

It was while he was with the 8th Battalion of the West Riding Regiment, on August 11th, 1917, that he won his Victoria Cross.

The action took place at Steinbeck Sidings on the Somme and the award was for most conspicuous bravery and indomitable resolution during the attack on a strongly held enemy position, his platoon having been checked by heavy machine-gun fire. He crawled through partially cut wire, dragging his Lewis gun with him and alone dealt with a strong party of the enemy, killing about 20 of them and thus covering the consolidation of the position taken up by his platoon.

Immediately afterwards, his Lewis gun was blown up by a bomb and three enemy rushed for him, but he shot them all with his revolver. Later, he shot several enemy snipers, exposing himself to heavy fire at the time.

On returning to his original post, he also brought back a wounded comrade under heavy fire, at risk of his own life. He displayed throughout an utter disregard of danger."

Later in the war, on June 19th, 1918, during a raid on Zillebreke, he was awarded the Distinguished Conduct Medal.

On 11th October, 1918, exactly a month before the armistice, he was badly wounded by being shot through both legs.

After the war, disabled now through the loss of a leg, he received help from The Sheffield Rotary Club who provided him with a bungalow and a pony and trap. However, his gallant service in the Great War had taken a dreadful toll on his health and he died of his war wounds in 1924, at the age of 27, leaving a widow and a three year old son. He is buried in the churchyard of All Saints Church, Ecclesall. The grave is shared with another family and the gravestone is lopsided and self-effacing. It is as if Sheffield is ashamed of having heroes!

His widow was cruelly affected by his death and was left in severe financial straits. The Government, in its wisdom, if it can be called that, refused to pay her a war widows pension! Their reasons were that because she hadn't married Mr Loosemore until after his war service had finished, and by that time he had received his wounds, she had married him knowing that his health was already damaged.

Of course this sort of offhand and "nit picking" attitude is a disgrace and it is easy to dismiss it as part of the hidebound outlook of the time and say that it couldn't happen today. But could it?

Lt. GEORGE LAMBERT V.C.

The gravestone, in Wardsend Cemetery, Owlerton, which carries the following inscription, is lying flat on the ground, but it was once upright. Whether it then fell or was pushed down flat or was purposely placed is difficult to decide. In either event, its prone position and the rampant weed growth in the cemetery make it very difficult to locate. I found it purely by accident while standing on it to photograph another grave nearby. I couldn't believe that it was the memorial to a holder of the Victoria Cross.

IN
MEMORY OF
GEORGE LAMBERT, VC
LIEUTENANT AND ADJUTANT.
84th REGIMENT.
WHO DIED AT SHEFFIELD
10th FEBRUARY 1860.
AGED 39 YEARS.
THIS TABLET IS ERECTED
BY HIS BROTHER OFFICERS.

George Lambert was born in December, 1819 in the small Irish town of Market Hill, County Armagh. He enlisted into the British Army on April 29th, 1842 and served in the Second Battalion, 84th Regiment of Foot (later to become the York & Lancaster Regiment). At the time he was a sergeant-major in India and it was for three actions, during the Indian Mutiny, that he was awarded his Victoria Cross. This award was gazetted in London on June 18th, 1858.

Although he remained in the army until his death, he had received a severe head wound from which he never fully recovered.

He was promoted to officer rank on December 12th, 1857 and when he died in Sheffield on 10th February, 1860, he was serving as a Lieutenant. He also held the Indian Mutiny Medal (1857-58) with clasp for the defence of Lucknow.

Once again I have been amazed at the cavalier attitude that Sheffield displays towards its heroes and great men. No history book that I have read which covers the history of former VC winners, nor local history books, mention his grave and its location in Wardsend Cemetery.

The following is information supplied by the York & Lancaster Regimental Museum, Rotherham:-

"Lambert, George, V.C. - Born at Market Hill, December, 1819. Served in Ranks June 6th, 1840, to December 11th, 1857; Ensign without purchase December 12th, 1857; Adjutant July 2nd, 1858; Lieutenant without purchase September 17th, 1858; Died in Sheffield, February 10th, 1860; Served in East Indies, August 8th, 1842, to September 2nd, 1859. Present at the following actions, viz:- Oonao and Busseerutgunge, July 29th, 1857; Busseerutgunge, August 5th, 1857; Boorbeakee Chowkee, August 12th, 1857; Bithoor, August 16th, 1857; Mungawar, September 21st, 1857; Alumbagh, September 23rd, 1857; Relief of Lucknow, September 25th, 1857; and subsequent seige, including the storming of Hirn Khana; Occupation of the Camp at Alumbagh; Seige and capture of Lucknow. Served with the Azimghur Field Force in all the minor Actions with that Column.

Served also in the Shahabad District until the suppression of the rebellion in that District; Severly wounded in the head at the relief of Lucknow, September 25th, 1857. Awarded the Victoria Cross for conspicuous gallantry in the field on July 29th, 1857, at the battle of Oonao; on August 16th, 1857, at Bithoor; and, on September 25th, at the relief of Lucknow. Medal and two clasps."

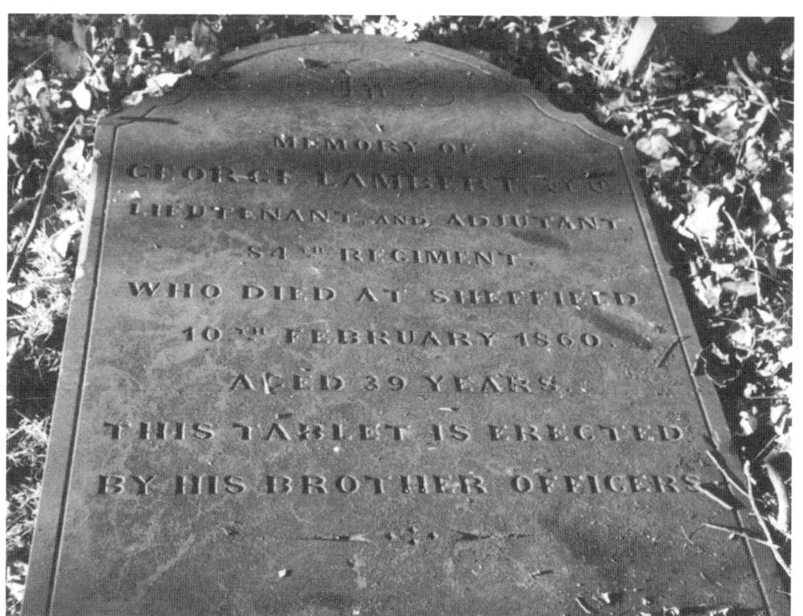

THE REV.
ARTHUR HERBERT PROCTOR V.C.

Although he was born in Bootle, Lancashire on 11th August, 1890, The Rev. Proctor spent some time in Sheffield and actually died here on 27th January, 1973.

During the First World War he served in the 1st / 5th Battalion, The King's (Liverpool) Regiment and was a private soldier at the time of his brave action. This took place near Ficheux, France on 4th June, 1916.

After the war, he studied for the church and was ordained into the priesthood in 1927. He once again involved himself in action during the Second World War, serving as an RAF chaplain. After his death in 1973, a memorial tablet was placed inside the crypt of Sheffield Cathedral.

I have been unable to find out any information as to the whereabouts of his grave, if he was buried, nor any other information about his family.

CHAPTER EIGHT

THEY SHALL NOT GROW OLD........

" When we, the Workers, all demand:
"What are we fighting for?
Then, then we'll end that stupid crime,
that devil's madness - War."

Robert William Service
1874-1958

SOON after I became interested in war graves, I became worried about one point - how many of the servicemen who were listed as killed in action on their graves, actually lay beneath the stones?

I wrote to the one place that I thought might know, The Imperial War Museum, and sure enough, they did. Below is a quote from the relevant part of their reply letter:-

"No British soldier who died abroad during the two World Wars was brought back to Great Britain for burial. The war graves that one sees in this country belong to those who died here, presumably though ill health, the results of wounds received on active service or in accidents. Sometimes one does see family graves which have reference to those killed abroad during the wars, but these are a memorial rather than the physical location of the body.

When the Imperial War Graves Commission was founded a decision was taken that all should be equal in death and consequently all bodies would be buried where they had died. This was to prevent those who could afford it bringing bodies back home for reburial while those who could not would have to suffer the double distress of losing a loved one and having no access to a grave."

Most wars begin in a ferment of madness fuelled by mobs of jubilant young men bawling patriotic songs, backed up by their women, or shouting slogans and swaggering with innocent bravado. That is before death joins the ranks and the pain, despair and suffering begins; before terror burrows into the brain and soft flesh cringes; before men begin to die!

Standard British War Gravestones

When it ends, as it must in time; when the guns cease firing, the random bombs stop falling and the flow of blood dries up, the material wounds are healed. Cities are rebuilt, enemies become allies and life returns to the uneasy truce that is modern civilization.

But so quickly does a modern battlefield regenerate itself that, within a few years, all that is left to drag unwilling memories back to the days of darkness and horror are the war memorials and the graves. They remain as the silent reminders of lost youth; the stupidity of men; the brave, but pointless sacrifices and the lives thrown away. They are the quiet accusers.

Every burial ground in Britain has its frosting of small, white regulation gravestones. Government designed, they are not pretty and tell little. Just the bare official particulars of number, rank and name; the date, the age and the arm of the services died for. Sometimes, the death is remembered by a few lines added prematurely to a family grave. Out of place and out of order.

It is often possible, if you know a little history, to remember what a date means. Some stand out starkly. July 1st, 1916 is a date which is seen very often and this is hardly surprising. It was the opening dreadful day of the Battle of the Somme. This day has gone down in history as the blackest day that the British Army has ever suffered. When the British barrage of heavy guns, which had been pounding the German trenches for days and nights on end, stopped, a huge mine was exploded beneath a section of the enemy trenches and, at 7.20am on a bright and sunny July morning, the British infantry rose from the relative safety of their trenches and began to walk slowly and in good order towards the Germans - the enemy who were supposed to have been so decimated and cowed by the long period of British shelling of their positions, that they would offer little, if any, resistance to the advancing British infantry. The generals, safe in their chateaux miles behind the front line, were once again proved dreadfully wrong!

When the carnage eased up with the coming of darkness and the butchery almost stopped, the British Army and its allies had a total casualty list of 57,470, mostly sustained in the first bloody hour of the battle. Of this list, 19,240 were either killed or died of their wounds. Apart from the men killed or wounded the worst of all was,"missing, believed killed in action" - the stilted Army phrase used in official reports when a young man was either blown to pieces, drowned in the seemingly bottomless stinking mud or blown out of the sky.

Today, at Thiepval, in Northern France, there is a desolate place which is dominated by a huge, stone-faced, brick-arched memorial. It is here that the names are carved of the 73,412 British servicemen, who were part of the Battle of the Somme which began on 1st July, 1916, and who have no known grave.

Never in the bloody history of warfare through the ages have so many men been sacrificed so pointlessly in such a short space of time, for so little gain. It is the nearest, I believe, that this world has come, so far, to Armageddon!

The first Military Service Act which became law in January, 1916, made liable for service all single men and childless widowers between the ages of 18 and 41. This was amended by six further Acts. The Act of 1918 permitted the extension of compulsory service to include men up to the age of 56 years and the final Act, passed in April, 1919, retained conscription for a further 12 months.

Although more than five and a half million men served in the British Army during the First World War, at the outbreak the army consisted of, including reservists and part-time territorials, 733,514 men. Between August, 1914 and December, 1915, enlistments numbered 2,466,719 and conscription between January, 1916 and November, 1918 brought in 2,504,183 men. Never before had an army had to cope with such numbers and they placed an obvious strain on the military machine.

Sheffield had, right at the beginning of the war, formed a City Battalion which became later the 12th (Service) Battalion of the York & Lancaster Regiment, which became part of the 94th Brigade together with the 1st and 2nd Barnsley Pals (13th & 14th Battalions York & Lancasters) and the Accrington Pals (11th Battalion, East Lancashires). All these young men were volunteers.

The break down of the casualty list for this disasterous first day of the Battle of the Somme makes grim reading:- Sheffield City Battalion - 512; Accrington Pals - 585; 1st Barnsley - 286; 2nd Barnsley - 275. The final total for the soldiers who were either killed instantly or who later died of their wounds was:- Sheffield City Battalion - 248, of whom 165 were never identified, so badly were they mutilated; Accrington Pals - 235; 1st Barnsley - 100; 2nd Barnsley - 110. Remember - this was one day of one battle, there was much more horror still to come!

There are understandably more First World War graves in the cemeteries of Sheffield than from the later world war, but both conflicts have bequeathed more than sufficient.

Slowly they are being forgotten as relatives age and die. Soon, it is possible to believe, they will all have eroded into nothing. Unless what doesn't bear thinking about happens, and a new crop of war graves appear.

None of the graves and monuments which follow are in any particular order. No-one who gives his life for his country, whether he understood what was happening or not, deserves more or less praise than any other victim of the madness.

Below is an obelisk which is in Wardsend Cemetery. This burial ground, which is at the end of Livesey Street, off Penistone Road, has been disused for many years and has recently begun to be cleared of the undergrowth which has appeared due to long neglect. This work is being tackled by members of a volunteer group who are very dedicated to the task, as are various other groups throughout the city, working in other burial grounds.

The square, tapered granite block which makes up this memorial stands very near to the path which has recently been laid and which gives access to the heart of the cemetery. It is engraved with the names of soldiers who died during peacetime, at Hillsborough Barracks, between the years 1866 and 1869. The stone is signed at the base:- F Ollerenshaw & Co.

The following inscription is taken from two adjacent sides of the obelisk. The other two sides are blank:-

THIS STONE IS ERECTED BY THE OFFICERS,
NON-COMMISSIONED OFFICERS AND MEN OF
THE 14th DEPOT BATTALION
TO THE MEMORY OF THE UNDERNAMED
OFFICER, SERGEANTS, CORPORALS,
DRUMMER AND PRIVATES
WHO DIED IN SHEFFIELD
IN 1866-67-68 AND 69.
MARCH. 1869.

STAFF-SURGEON D.C.TAYLOR M.D.
COLOUR SERGEANT
WILLIAM BOWDEN 1st. Battn. 19th Reg.
COLOUR SERGEANT
JOHN BAILEY 2nd-19th.
COLOUR SERGEANT
WILLIAM NEWELL 2nd-24th.
SERGEANT THOMAS HAVILAND
1st-24th.
SERGEANT WILLIAM ROBERTS
1st-24th.
CORPORAL JOHN ARNOLD
1st-24th.
CORPORAL MAURICE CONNELL
2nd-19th.
CORPORAL HENRY SCOTT
1st-6th.
DRUMMER PATRICK PEARCE
55th.

PRIVATES

WILM. DORAN 1st-19th Reg.
JOHN OSBORN 1st-19th.
J. STEVENSON 1st-24th.
WILM. DERRY 1st-24th.
J.H.CLEVELAND 1st-24th.
JAMES MONORGAN 1st-24th.
SQUIRE PARKIN 1st-24th.
CHARLES COLLINGE 1st-24th.
WILM. BROWN 1st-24th.
JOHN HURST 1st-24th.
GEORGE PICKETT 1st-24th.
JAMES DEAN 2nd-6th.

ALFRED POWELL 2nd-24th.
GEORGE LEMON 2nd-24th.
EDWARD PRICE 2nd-24th.
HAMPSON WALSH 33rd.
PETER SMYTH 51st.
LEVI CROSBY 51st.
THOMAS KELLY 55th.
CHARLES BRIGHTMORE 55th.
JOHN IVILL 55th.
JOHN DALY 55th.
JAMES DOE 55th.

Below is part of the inscription on a grave in Wardsend Cemetery, which commemorates the death of a soldier who was killed on 1st July, 1916, the first day of the Battle of the Somme. He was one of the many who walked into the machine-gun fire on that July day. Private Smout was probably serving with the 8th Battalion, 8th Division which were fighting in the Authville Wood / Ovillers area of the front line. The Y & L on the tombstone stands for the York & Lancaster Regiment. His parents were Edward and Martha Hannah Smout, who died on March 14th, 1925 and June 16th, 1934 respectively.

PTE. WILLIAM T. SMOUT. Y & L.
SON OF THE ABOVE,
KILLED IN ACTION IN FRANCE JULY 1st. 1916
AGED 30 YEARS.

This gravestone in Wardsend Cemetery, is very large for just a single set of inscriptions. Was he expecting someone else to join him in the same plot?

IN MEMORY OF
SERGEANT HENRY ALEXANDER McCOMBIE
1st BRIGADE ROYAL ARTILLERY
WHO DIED APRIL 19th. 1874.
AGED 39 YEARS.

The soldier who is remembered on this gravestone in Tinsley Park Cemetery, actually died over two months after the Armistice began which ended the First World War - the actual documents which ended the war and which set out the terms by which the German forces and their allies surrendered were not signed until 28th June, 1919 at Versailles. Presumably he died either of wounds or from the effects of gas. The stone is a standard British war grave design.

TR/5 223339 PRIVATE
L.L. MARSH
KINGS OWN YORKSHIRE L.I.
29th JANUARY, 1919.

This grave in Tinsley Park Cemetery tells of a family tragedy which must have been all too common at that time. It involves the deaths of three young people from the same family - a young father killed very early on in the First World War, whose death was followed two months later by that of his six month old daughter. Finally, his brother - in - law was killed less than three months before the end of hostilities. How must Mary Ann Denman have felt? First her husband, then her daughter and then her brother all dead within three years.

Sgt. JOHN EDWARD
THE BELOVED HUSBAND OF
MARY ANN DENMAN
WHO DIED IN BELGIUM AUG. 18th 1815
AGED 22 YEARS
ALSO MARY ANN
BELOVED CHILD OF THE ABOVE
WHO DIED OCT. 16th 1915
AGED 6 MONTHS
ALSO PTE. JAMES HODGSON K.O.Y.L.I.
THE BELOVED SON OF
JAMES &MARGARET HODGSON
& BROTHER OF Mrs M.A. DENMAN
KILLED IN FRANCE AUG 27th 1918
AGED 21 YEARS

(Private Hodgson served in the Kings Own Yorkshire Light Infantry)

There is a Canadian Air Force grave in Tinsley Park Cemetery. How he came to be buried here is not known. He would have died of wounds received.

R. 97987 FLIGHT SERGEANT
R.P. DAVIES
PILOT
ROYAL CANADIAN AIR FORCE
11th AUGUST 1942 AGED 21.

Another airman, this time from the Royal Air Force, is remembered on a grave nearby and he had the worst kind of luck as he died on Christmas Day. This was after the end of the Second World War, so it must be assumed that he died of his wounds.

626380 LDG. AIRCRAFTMAN
D. GARVIN
ROYAL AIR FORCE
25th DECEMBER, 1945. AGED 26

The war memorial in Tinsley Park Cemetery, which stands at its highest part, is a plain stone cross standing on a two step octagonal stone base. The inscription, which is for the First World War dead only and is short and simple, reads:-

TO THE
HONOURED
MEMORY
OF THOSE
SAILORS
AND SOLDIERS
WHO
GAVE THEIR
LIVES
FOR THEIR
COUNTRY
IN THE GREAT
WAR
1914 - 1918 AND
WHO
LIE BURIED IN
THIS CEMETERY

The following three graves in Intake Cemetery are all marked with standard British war gravestones. The first grave is unusual in that it commemorates two men who were probably brothers serving in different arms of the forces.

1062688 SERGEANT
T.R.THOMPSON
WIRELESS OPERATOR/AIR GUNNER
ROYAL AIR FORCE
4th AUGUST 1942 AGE 21

ALSO TO THE MEMORY OF
A.B. RONALD THOMPSON RN.
BURIED AT SEA
11th JUNE 1944

Adjacent to the above grave is another commemorating a W.Op/AG

650284 FLIGHT SERGEANT
R.P.GILLOT
WIRELESS OPERATOR/AIR GUNNER
ROYAL AIR FORCE
12th JULY 1942 AGE 22
HE DIED THAT WE MIGHT LIVE

The final grave in this group is yet again a W.Op/AG. The short verse at the end of the inscription is not one that I have come across before. It is very perceptive.

1061093 SERGEANT
R. LEYLAND
WIRELESS OPERATOR/AIR GUNNER
ROYAL AIR FORCE
20th MARCH 1942 AGE 20
HE SPED THROUGH LIFE
ON A SLEDGE OF JOY
HE DIED AS A MAN
BUT WAS ONLY A BOY

This grave, in Ecclesall Churchyard, seems, at first glance, to be nothing more than a family grave commemorating the lives of four people, one of them a serving soldier. But on closer inspection it has rather sad features.

Lieut. Bradbury didn't die in action, but was killed in an accident. Although only 25 years old, he was already a qualified bachelor of both medicine and surgery and must have been a very gifted young man.

There is something else, even more tragic about this grave. Also remembered is Lieut. Bradbury's fiancee, Mary Holmes. She died just three weeks after his death. She was 21 years old. According to information given to me by one of the small team of volunteer workers who tidy up the churchyard, both these young people died as the result of a house fire.

IN LOVING
MEMORY OF
LIEUT. DAN BRADBURY M.B., Ch. B.
MO1939/40. 71st FIELD REGIMENT. R.A.
PASSED ON AS THE RESULT OF AN ACCIDENT
DECEMBER 1st 1940 AGED 25 YEARS
ALSO
MARY HOLMES FIANCEE OF THE ABOVE
PASSED ON DECEMBER 22nd 1940
AGED 21 YEARS

(The other two people on the gravestone are Dan Bradbury's parents)

This is a brass plaque on the wall of Middlewood Church which is a Victorian listed building and is, along with a few of the hospital buildings, all that is left of what was once a very large mental hospital complex. During the war years of this century, it was used as a hospital for the wounded and for gas victims.

IN MEMORY
OF
ATT. J WAREHAM
COLDSTREAM GUARDS
WHO GAVE HIS LIFE
FOR HIS COUNTRY
IN THE SOUTH AFRICAN WAR
1899

Here is another victim of the insanity of the Battle of the Somme. He was in the Sheffield City Battalion and his grave is in Ecclesall Churchyard:-

....ALSO OF
SERGEANT
WALTER
THOMPSON
SON OF THE
ABOVE
(LATE CITY
BATTALION)
WHO FELL IN
ACTION IN
FRANCE
JULY 1st 1916
AGED 27 YEARS

There are a number of small, square stone plaques set high into the wall of the Methodist Church, Norfolk Hill, Grenoside. Some are in memory of soldiers who gave their lives in the First World War. The inscriptions are as follows:-

IN LOVING MEMORY
OF WALTER
SON OF ALBERT
AND ELLEN LOWE
AND HUSBAND OF
AMELIA LOWE
DIED OF WOUNDS
IN FRANCE
AUGUST 25th 1918
AGED 27 YEARS

The soldiers named in these first two memorials appear to have been brothers.

IN LOVING MEMORY
OF ARTHUR
SON OF ALBERT
AND ELLEN LOWE
PRESUMED KILLED
IN FRANCE
JUNE 29th 1917
AGED 32 YEARS

IN LOVING MEMORY OF
ALLAN
ONLY SON OF
J. AND J. A. FIRTH
KILLED IN ACTION
AT L'EPINETTE
FRANCE
APRIL 13th 1918
AGED 20 YEARS

IN
LOVING MEMORY
OF
Ld BAILEY
WHO DIED OF WOUNDS
IN FRANCE
AUGUST 5th 1917
AGED 34 YEARS

The young man commemorated on the following grave, in Shiregreen Cemetery, gave his life for his country in 1956. It is difficult to think where in the world, in that period of history, British soldiers were fighting and dying, unless it was in the Far East in somewhere like Malaya or Kenya.

Also named on the family grave are his parents and one of their grandchildren who died aged only six weeks old.

.....ALSO THEIR SON ROY,
KILLED ON ACTIVE SERVICE
28th SEPT. 1956. AGED 19.

Outside Sheffield Cathedral, on the forecourt, there is a square, stainless steel plaque on a small marble base.

IN REMEMBERANCE
OF THOSE WHO LOST THEIR LIVES
ON HMS 'SHEFFIELD'
DURING THE FALKLANDS CONFLICT
PLACED BY SHEFFIELD JUNIOR
CHAMBER OF COMMERCE
SIMULTANEOUSLY WITH THE
JUNIOR CHAMBERS OF
COVENTRY, LIVERPOOL, PLYMOUTH,
PORTSMOUTH AND SOUTHAMPTON
11th NOVEMBER 1982

These two graves are in Shiregreen Cemetery and commemorate a soldier and an airman from the Second World War

TREASURED MEMORIES OF
JACK. LIEUT. R.A.
DEARLY LOVED ONLY SON OF
SYDNEY W. AND EVA BOWLES
DIED JUNE 15th 1944,
AGED 24 YEARS.
AFTER SERVICE IN THE CENTRAL
MEDITERRANEAN FORCES.

IN LOVING MEMORY OF
L.A.C. BOB MARRIOTT RAF.
KILLED ON ACTIVE SERVICE
12th FEBRUARY 1942
AGED 20 YEARS.

Inside the foyer of Sheffield Town Hall, on the left hand wall, there is a large rectangular memorial to the South African (Boer) War. The outside surround of bronze is heavily decorated with Yorkshire roses and heraldic symbols. The centre rectangular piece is made of polished marble. On this part of the memorial, at the top left hand corner, is the coat of arms of the City of Sheffield and in the centre and on the right hand portions are the following inscriptions -

The centre column:-

AT A MONTHLY MEETING OF THE COUNCIL OF THE CITY OF SHEFFIELD HELD AT THE TOWN HALL, SHEFFIELD ON WEDNESDAY THE TENTH DAY OF SEPTEMBER 1902,

THE RIGHT HONOURABLE GEORGE SENIOR, LORD MAYOR, IN THE CHAIR, IT WAS MOVED BY THE LORD MAYOR, SECONDED BY Mr ALDERMAN CLEGG, AND CARRIED UNANIMOUSLY:-

THAT THIS COUNCIL DESIRE AND RESOLVE TO PLACE ON RECORD, THEIR APPRECIATION AND RECOGNITION OF THE LOYAL SERVICES RENDERED TO THEIR COUNTRY BY THE VOLUNTEERS,

The right hand column:-

AMBULANCEMEN, AND TELEGRAPHISTS OF SHEFFIELD, WHO VOLUNTEERED AND WENT OUT ON ACTIVE SERVICE WITH HIS MAJESTY'S ARMY IN SOUTH AFRICA, AND THAT THEIR NAMES BE INSCRIBED ON THE MINUTES OF THIS COUNCIL, AND THAT A COPY OF THIS RESOLUTION, SIGNED BY THE LORD MAYOR, BE PRESENTED TO EACH SUCH VOLUNTEER. THE CORPORATE COMMON SEAL OF THE LORD MAYOR, ALDERMEN AND CITIZENS OF THE CITY OF SHEFFIELD WAS HEREUNTO AFFIXED IN THE PRESENCE OF

(The signature of the Lord Mayor)

(The signature of the Town Clerk)

(The seal of the Lord Mayor)

Beneath these inscriptions, in ten columns, are the names, stretching right across the marble part of the memorial, of all the volunteers who served in the Army during the Boer War. There are 403 such names. The men served in The Royal Engineers; The First Telegraph Battalion; The Imperial Yeomanry; The First West Yorks Royal Engineers (Volunteers); The First Volunteer Battalion of the York and Lancaster Regiment and The St. John Ambulance Brigade (Sheffield Corps).

This grave is in Wadsley Churchyard. The stone is attractive, but is almost buried in the undergrowth, and the top is decorated with blacksmiths equipment carved into the granite. Although this soldier seems to have died of natural causes, I felt that the combination of poem and gravestone merited his inclusion in this section.

IN MEMORY OF
SAMUEL, SON OF
SAMUEL AND AMELIA JEPSON,
OF WADSLEY. WHO DIED MARCH 6th 1863,
AGED 45 YEARS.
HE WAS SERGEANT FARRIER TO THE
SIXTEENTH LANCERS, TWENTY YEARS
AND SIX MONTHS.
THE TIRED SOLDIER BOLD AND BRAVE,
NOW RESTS HIS WEARY FEET,
UNTO THE SHELTER OF THE GRAVE,
(H)AS MADE A SAFE RETREAT
BILLETED HER(E) BY DEATH;
IN ORDERS TO REMAIN;
UNTIL THE LAST TRUMPET SHALL SOUND,
ARISE AND MARCH AGAIN.

Also buried in the grave are his parents, Samuel and Amelia.

In the graveyard of St. John's Church, Chapeltown, there is a grave which commemorates a man who was part of the Duke of Wellington's Army which fought the Peninsular Wars against Napoleon Bonaparte. As every schoolboy used to know, this series of wars culminated in victory for the British and their allies at the Battle of Waterloo, near the village of that name in Belgium, in 1815. It was, like most pitched battles of those wars, a bloody affair and John Hird was fortunate to be able to return to his native Yorkshire and live to what even today is considered to be a "ripe old age".

Also remembered on the grave are his son, daughter-in-law and grand-daughter, but the stone is becoming so badly eroded by the elements that dates and ages are impossible to read. Once again an important historical item is being lost to Sheffield through neglect and disinterest.

IN LOVING
MEMORY OF
JOHN HIRD
WHO DIED JUNE 30th 1873,
AGED 83 YEARS.
HE SERVED HIS KING & COUNTRY
ON THE FIELD OF WATERLOO.

CHAPTER NINE

STAND AND DELIVER

"Little thieves we hang; great ones we let go free."

German proverb

THEY may have been anti-social criminals, thieves and robbers, but highwaymen still retain, even in these cynical days, a certain aura of romance. Most of this probably stems from the romantic legends, boosted by films, which, true or false, were built up around Britain's most famous highwayman, Dick Turpin.

Sheffield's own member of this fraternity wasn't in the same league as Turpin and correspondingly doesn't have the widespread fame that Turpin enjoys, nor of others whose names are still fairly well known like Jack Shepherd, a well known jail breaker. In fact, as far as success went, Spence Broughton wasn't very good at it and, as a failure, he ended his life on a gibbet entertaining the crowds.

Most history books which cover Sheffield in any depth have a section on the town's criminals. Broughton usually gets a mention and quite often these accounts differ or are identical in their mistakes.

I have delved deeper than perhaps most local historians and have come up with what I feel may well be a fairly accurate account of Spence Broughton's career, such as it was. There may be errors, I will be the first to admit, but then he wasn't famous enough for any in-depth records to have been written at the time.

Spence Broughton was born into the family of a small Lincolnshire farmer. His father was by no means a wealthy man, but he ensured that his son was as well educated as he could afford and that he married as well as was possible for someone of his class.

Thus, by the time he was 20 years old, he was married and working his own small farm near Sleaford, Lincolnshire. His wife, about whom little is known, had some money and for a while things appeared to be set fair for a quiet and reasonably prosperous, if dull, life.

Broughton had a flaw, however - he was a spendthrift with a weakness for strong drink and gambling. It was to prove his downfall. The farm either failed or became too boring and Broughton left the area to travel round the country in search, perhaps, of adventure. He was, after all, still a young man.

He spent some time in Sheffield where he settled in New Street, in the West Bar area of the town which at that period of the 18th century was "where it all happened". He must have mixed freely with members of Sheffield's criminal underclass and one of the men he associated with was John Oxley.

The pair left for London and there they teamed up with Thomas Shaw and John Close, a fellow Sheffielder. These last two men were partners in a gaming club. This doesn't appear to have been very profitable as the quartet were never very well off and it was this pressing need for money, together with Oxley's knowledge of the Sheffield to Rotherham Post Office routine (he had once been employed for a short time as a "post boy" responsible for the Rotherham Mail) which led to their plan to rob the mail.

As Broughton and Oxley had recent local knowledge, it was agreed that they would return to Sheffield and commit the robbery. They first travelled to Nottingham where they put up for the night and the following day they walked to Chesterfield, where they stayed the night at The Three Cranes Inn.

The next day, 29th January, 1791, they walked to Sheffield and then down Attercliffe Common, at that time a very barren and lonely area of the town's outskirts. It was there that they planned to apprehend and rob the mail.

The security employed by the Post Office was poor and the mail was carried by a 13 year old boy named George Lesley, who was easily overpowered and tied up in a field beside the road. The mail bag was taken and the two men were soon on their way to Mansfield.

It wasn't a brilliant piece of villainy. The boy was loosely tied and soon escaped; his horse was tied up nearby and he had no trouble in riding off to raise the alarm. The mail bag, when the two men opened it, contained little of value apart from a French Bill of Exchange worth £124. This sum of money may have been worth far more than it is today, but it was hardly enough to risk the hangman's rope.

After reaching Mansfield on 30th January, the pair split up. Broughton was suffering from foot trouble brought on, no doubt, by the prolonged spells of walking and was lame. He remained in Mansfield, while Oxley, bill of exchange in his pocket, pushed on to London. Broughton seemed to have been a very trusting, or perhaps naive, young man.

By the time Oxley reached London and managed to cash the bill, the news of the robbery was widespread due to an announcement published on 4th February in the Sheffield Advertiser newspaper.

On his recovery, Broughton followed his accomplice to London and found him gone. He discovered that Oxley had several days' start on him at the gaming tables and, having lost heavily, had decamped to Leicester with what remained of the bill of exchange. Broughton followed him and managed to squeeze £40 from his partner which, no doubt, soon followed the rest.

Once more hard pressed for cash and boosted up by the simplicity of their first venture, the pair carried out a further two robberies. The first was the Aylesbury Mail on 28th May, 1791, which was an absolute fiasco. Not only did they gain nothing, but the robbery actually cost them around £15 to set up! The second escapade was similar to the first one and was carried out on the Cambridge Mail. This was, as far as the thieves were concerned, the jackpot. Although a fairly loose estimate was given, it was thought that they got away with between £5,000 and £10,000.

It is not known what part in these robberies was taken by Shaw and Close, but they had some involvement as it is obvious from later events that they shared part of the proceeds from at least the last robbery.

That was the end of the criminal career of Spence Broughton.

Oxley was the first of the four to be arrested. This, it is said, was following a report from a boy who saw him twice within a few days pay for shop purchases with large denomination banknotes. Oxley, true to the code, shopped his friends.

When Shaw was accosted, he was found to be in possession of a large sum of money for someone in his circumstances. Close and Broughton were also soon arrested. These arrests were carried out by the then police force, The Bow Street Runners, the forerunner of the force later set up by Sir Robert Peel.

Only Broughton and Oxley, for some reason, were sufficiently implicated in the robberies to be held, however, and Close and Shaw were freed. Although it was never proved, it was believed at the time that Oxley, in return for "helping" the police, was later allowed to escape. It was said that his cell window was left insecure and that a ladder was placed nearby. In any event, he did the sensible thing and, although handcuffed, he escaped into the night leaving Broughton alone to face the music.

Broughton was transferred to York where he stood trial at the assizes on 24th March, 1792. He was found guilty after a trial which barely lasted three hours and sentenced to hang. After passing the sentence of death, the judge instructed that " his body was unworthy of heaven or earth and that it should be suspended between to be buffeted by winds and storm".

Broughton sweated out the mandatory three Sundays' wait and was finally swung into space at York Tyburn on Saturday, 14th April, 1792. His final words, something the large crowds, who loved a good execution and attended in their thousands, were always keen to hear, were not memorable. He merely said " that he forgave the world, except Shaw and wished he was with him". What he had especially against Shaw is not known - it was Oxley who deserted him!

His wretched body, now coated in tar and pitch to prevent it rotting too quickly, was returned to Sheffield. It was rivetted into an iron cage and suspended from a wooden gibbet which had been especially made and erected on Attercliffe Common near to the scene of his first crime. It was to stay there, swaying in the breeze and stinking, for many, some say as many as 35, years.

Spence Broughton's career as a highway robber lasted not quite 15 months.

Oxley returned to the Sheffield area and, in spite of a £100 reward for his capture, was never seen alive again and his body, starved and emaciated, was found in either late January or early February, 1793, on Loxley Moor.

These are the facts of Broughton's career as accurately as I can piece them together. After his execution there were, of course, many folk stories and tales. These can be believed or taken with the proverbial " pinch of salt".

One tale was that bones from his body were sold to the ghouls who drank in The Harrow public house, which was near the gibbet. Another story was that Swinton Pottery obtained a piece of bone, a knuckle, ground it up, mixed it with clay and fired a drinking mug out of the resulting mixture. Bone china? There was even a tale about a mysterious veiled woman in black who was reputed to have been Broughton's wife and who watched his body being hoisted up on to the gibbet from an upstairs room of The Harrow.

All this is good stuff, but probably untrue. What is true, however, is that a local newspaper, The Sheffield Local Register, published an account, on 3rd May, 1867, concerning the rediscovery of the remains of the gibbet. Apparently a man named Holroyd was digging new cellars on a site opposite The Yellow Lion public house, Clifton Street - I belive that this is the former Harrow public house under a different name - when he found an upright shaft of seasoned black oak which had been passed through and bolted to a large wooden frame, all of which had been solidly buried in the ground. These were the remains of Broughton's gibbet which had been made 75 years earlier by a man named Gregory. It was well known that the gibbet post had been sawn down many years earlier by the new owner of the land on which it stood, Mr Henry Sorby of Woodburn.

Sheffield has never forgotten this minor, and to a large extent, unsuccessful villain. Not only do we have Broughton Lane and the memorial plaque pictured here, but a local public house, once reasonably known as the Railway, then The Stadium, has now joined the "heritage" trail and become The Noose & Gibbet!

Oh, yes. A minor bus company which operates in Sheffield, once and perhaps still does, own a bus named Spence Broughton.

CHAPTER TEN

NOT BY ACCIDENT

"Other sins only speak, murder shrieks out."

John Webster c1580-c1625

HIS chapter is mercifully short and if it had not been for the lasting impression that these graves left with me, I should not have included it at all.

This was the first, and hopefully, the last time that I have ever stood and looked down at the graves of three murder victims. It was an experience which I would far rather forget if I could. The Jewish cemetery on the outskirts of Ecclesfield, where I found the three black marble graves one late autumn afternoon, was chilly and overcast and I felt a huge oppressive sadness and sense of unease.

There cannot be many people in Sheffield and probably further afield who did not hear about these murders in 1983. It was a vicious and nasty crime carried out by a cruel and brutal man. Although the man, Arthur Hutchinson, who committed the murders and the rape, was caught soon afterwards and jailed for 18 years, the memories, although perhaps fading with the passing of the years, will stay for a long time in the minds of the people.

It had been a happy, family occasion, a wedding, on an autumn day in late October. The house in Dore Road, one of the wealthier suburbs of Sheffield, was empty of all, but four family members, father, mother and two of their children.

Hutchinson, already a fugitive from the police, broke into the house, stabbed to death three of the family, the parents and son, and brutally sexually assaulted the daughter. It was a bloody and pointlessly vicious crime which robbed the city of three valuable and inoffensive citizens and ruined the life of a fourth.

The three tombs stand in a line; the inscription on the one on the left reads:-

IN LOVING MEMORY OF
RICHARD GORDON LAITNER
WHOSE LIFE TRAGICALLY ENDED
24th OCTOBER 1983 AGED 28.
HIS LOYALTY WILL ALWAYS BE REMEMBERED
HOW GREAT HIS POTENTIAL
SO GENEROUS HIS HEART.

The inscription on the centre grave is:-

IN LOVING MEMORY OF
Dr. AVRIL MIRRIE LAITNER
WHOSE LIFE TRAGICALLY ENDED
24th OCTOBER 1983 AGED 54.
HER LOVING CARE WILL ALWAYS BE REMEMBERED
BEQUEATHING MEMORIES AND
PRECIOUS THOUGHTS
THAT SHALL NOT DIE AND
CANNOT BE DESTROYED.

The inscription on the right hand grave is:-

IN LOVING MEMORY OF
BASIL GORDON LAITNER
WHOSE LIFE TRAGICALLY ENDED
24th OCTOBER 1983 AGED 59.
HIS DEVOTION WILL ALWAYS BE REMEMBERED
A MAN WHO WAS GENTLE
CARING AND JUST.

There is nothing else to say. May they rest in the peace that was denied them that autumn evening in October 1983.

CHAPTER ELEVEN

THE FINAL ARRESTING PLACE

***"To be wise by rule and by experience
are utterly opposite principles;
so that he who is used to one
is unfit for the other."***

***Francis Bacon (Lord Verulam and Viscount St. Albans)
1561 - 1626***

THE monument which follows, which is in the General Cemetery, is to Thomas Raynor, who was Chief Constable of Sheffield in the 19th Century. It is a large, square, granite memorial which would have been fitting to his status in the city. As Chief Constable of the Borough of Sheffield, he would have been an important man with wide ranging powers. This was long before the local police forces of the towns in South Yorkshire amalgamated to form the South Yorkshire Police Force that is in place today. The tribute at the bottom of the inscription could well be slightly tongue in cheek!

SACRED
TO THE MEMORY
OF
THOMAS RAYNOR,
LATE CHIEF CONSTABLE OF
THE BOROUGH OF SHEFFIELD.
WHO DIED NOVEMBER 17th 1860.
AGED 73 YEARS.
ESTEEMED BY HIS FRIENDS
AND GREATLY RESPECTED
BY THE PUBLIC.

IN AFFECTIONATE
REMEMBERANCE OF
STEPHEN PEARSON,
POLICE CONSTABLE,
THE BELOVED HUSBAND OF
HANNAH PEARSON,
WHO WAS STABBED IN CASTLE STREET
SEPTEMBER 10th 1891,
AND DIED JUNE 18th 1892,
AGED 40 YEARS.

This grave with its attractively designed stone, is at the top part of the General Cemetery. It commemorates the death of a policeman at the other end of the promotion ladder. This report is from a local newspaper and was written at the time of the incident:-

THE STABBING OF A SHEFFIELD POLICEMAN

"Stephen Pearson, the constable who was stabbed in the face while on duty in Castle Street early yesterday morning, is now considered out of danger, but serious fears were entertained about him for a few hours after his admission to hospital. He fell down insensible in the Charge Office from loss of blood, just after saying he had been stabbed. After his wound had been stitched up he became delirious, and two members of the police force were fetched to prevent him tearing the wound open.

It appears that Peter Byrne, the navvy who committed the outrage, was found by Pearson lying asleep in the Haymarket. When he was roused up he used some very bad language, and only went away on being told that he would be locked up if he did not. Half an hour later, while Pearson was standing in Castle Street, Byrne came up to him, began to threaten, and suddenly produced a big clasp knife. The blade was open and the navvy drove it with great violence into the constable's right jaw. A man named Booth saw the outrage, and if he had not been there at the moment there can be no telling what further injury would have been inflicted on Pearson. Byrne threw down the knife with an oath and quietly submitted to being taken to the Police Office."

Byrne had been working on the Manchester Ship Canal. When in court later, charged with maliciously wounding Constable Pearson, he was remanded in custody for eight days. In those days his probable sentence would have been several years' hard labour - but then, as a navvy, he was used to that!

Constable Pearson died nine months after being stabbed. It is probably worth wondering whether the stabbing incident was actually the cause of his death?

The following grave is in the Church of England section of Walkley Cemetery. It is extremely beautifully carved, but unfortunately will soon be covered by the ivy which is already beginning its relentless climb up the face of the stone. I could have put this grave in the chapter which concerns war dead, as two sons of the police superintendent were killed in the First World War. I decided on this chapter simply because there are far more war graves than dead policemen.

I have found an account in the Sheffield Daily Independant, dated October 26th, 1911, which gives a fairly detailed summary of Mr Andrew's life and career. I have only included the first and most important part of the account:-

"A painful surprise was created in the Sheffield Police Force yesterday by the receipt of a wire (telegram) from the Chief Constable of Douglas (Isle of Man) that Supt. Frederick Andrew, Chief of the Detective Department, had died in the Manx capital. He had been in hospital there with a broken ankle, but none was prepared for this sad news. Five weeks ago he went to Douglas for a holiday, accompanied by his wife, and as he had not visited the place since spending his honeymoon there, he announced to his colleagues that he was off for his second honeymoon. After being there a week he accidentally slipped on the asphalt in the hotel grounds and broke a bone in his ankle. He had been confined to hospital since, but he suffered no pain, and was quite cheerful. The cause of death is stated to be heart disease. It is a singular fact that previously he had not lost a days duty through illness."

A brief resumé of Supt. Andrew's career tells that he was born in Grantham, but had lived in Sheffield for many years. Previous to joining the police force, where he had served for 26 years, he was a joiner. Once in the force, he served for eight years as a beat constable before being promoted to detective sergeant. Three years later he was again in uniform as a sub-inspector and he was made full inspector four years after that. In this rank he was based at West Bar Station. In 1906, he was made chief inspector and soon after that, in 1907, he succeeded to the post of Superintendent of the Detective Department.

The Sheffield Daily Independent said:-

"It is no idle flattery to say that he was one of the ablest police officials in the country, and popular on all sides. One of his most striking characteristics was his keen insight into human nature. This, coupled with an extensive knowledge of police procedure, a wonderful memory for faces and facts, and initiative power, made him the capable officer he was."

His son, Joseph, died on the first day of the Battle of the Somme and his three line dedication includes the dreadful phrase, "Reported Missing!"

IN AFFECTIONATE REMEMBERANCE
OF FREDERICK ANDREW,
LATE DETECTIVE SUPERINTENDENT
SHEFFIELD CITY POLICE,
WHO DIED OCT. 25th 1911, AGED 48 YEARS.
"IN THE MIDST OF LIFE WE ARE IN DEATH"
ALSO IN MEMORY OF
L/CPL JOSEPH ANDREW,
No. 577 12th Y &L REPORTED MISSING
JULY 1st 1916, AGED 21 YEARS.
AND GUNNER JOHN ANDREW,
No. 213299. 86th BRIGADE R.F.A.KILLED IN ACTION
MARCH 21st 1918,
AGED 20 YEARS.
SONS OF THE ABOVE
FREDk AND SARAH ANN ANDREW.

This gravestone, in Wardsend Cemetery, is one of two which mark the graves of, or are in memory of, a large number of members of the Moores family.

IN AFFECTIONATE REMEMBERANCE
OF JOHN MOORES,
SENIOR INSPECTOR OF THE
SHEFFIELD BOROUGH POLICE,
BORN SEPTEMBER 15th, 1819,
DIED APRIL 23rd, 1885.
AT REST.

ALSO OF HANNAH MOORES,
WIFE OF THE ABOVE,
BORN JANUARY 2nd, 1823,
DIED JUNE 22nd, 1894.
"PEACE, PERFECT PEACE."
ALSO OF JOHN, THE BELOVED HUSBAND OF
MARIA FRANCES MOORES, AND SON OF THE ABOVE,
(OF THE CITY POLICE FORCE)
WHO DIED FEBRUARY 3rd, 1898,
AGED 41 YEARS.
ALSO OF FRED, THEIR SON,
WHO DIED IN INFANCY.

The other identical family stone is inscribed with the names of eight other family members, five of whom died in infancy.

The grave of this policeman is in Burngreave Cemetery and is inscribed:-

IN LOVING MEMORY
WILLIAM SMITH,
(LATE POLICE INSPECTOR)
THE BELOVED HUSBAND OF
JANE SMITH,
WHO DIED AUGUST 19th 1902,
AGED 51 YEARS.
ALSO OF THE ABOVE NAMED
JANE SMITH,
WHO DIED MARCH 5th 1933,
AGED 80 YEARS.

Also on the grave are inscriptions commemorating the son and daughter of the above.

SACRED TO THE MEMORY OF
JAMES WILSON,
LATE INSPECTOR OF THE SHEFFIELD POLICE
FORCE FOR A NUMBER OF YEARS
WHO DIED JANUARY 4th 1883,
AGED 77 YEARS.
"NOT DEAD BUT SLEEPING."

This addition to the chapter on policemen really has no place here as it represents the "other side of the fence", but the man mentioned here was used to close contact with the law!

Few of the inhabitants of Sheffield will not have heard of the Mooney Gang and Sheffield's gang wars. George Mooney, was the leader of that gang.

Born in Sheffield in the 1890's, but of Irish extraction, Mooney is still remembered for his criminal activities. His gang members were mostly based in the West Bar area of the city in the 1920's and were at their criminal peak between about 1923 and when they were broken up in 1928.

The passing years have glossed over the violence and brutality of the gang war which flared up between Mooney's gang and the rival Park Hill Brigade and now those years are looked back on or spoken of with an almost parochial pride; there have even been buses named after them.

When the facts are considered, they shouldn't be so venerated, for those few years were nothing more than a clash between rival mobs of, for the most part, work-shy, greedy and brutal minor criminals.

The basis of the feud was the battle for control of a "tossing ring" situated at Skye Edge. This was an illegal, but extremely lucrative source of income first for the Mooney Gang and then the Park Hill Brigade. Tossing rings were formed so that the gamblers of the town, mostly unemployed steel or cutlery workers, could chance their luck on the old game of pitch and toss. This was played with two coins, usually half-pennies, which were placed on the ends of the first two fingers of one hand and then tossed into the air. The resulting combination of "heads" or "tails" when the coins landed decided the outcome of the bets. A simple game which literally "coined" money for the controllers of the ring.

George Mooney was never much more than a minor villain. He joined the Army at the outbreak of the First World War, became a corporal and then spent most of the duration of the hostilities absent without leave and on the dodge from the military police. During his life he lived at various addresses in Sheffield - Trinity Street, Corporation Street (the house he lived in there was demolished along with the rest of the corner block in July, 1997), and Rose Street. He collected an impressive string of convictions over the course of the years and spent several periods behind bars.

When the Sheffield gangs were broken up by Captain Sillitoe's Flying Squad in 1928, Mooney spent the rest of his life in a fairly quiet and law abiding way. He was a familiar sight on the racecourses and dog tracks of the north of England where he often stood as a bookmaker under the name of George Barratt. He died on 22nd June, 1961.

Members of the original Mooney gang included:- John Thomas, George's brother, John James Murphy, Peter Winsey, Tommy Rippon, Frank Kidnew, who later defected to the Park Brigade, Albert Foster and Bill Naughton.

The inscription on the rather shabby and uncared for grave, which is tucked away in a quiet part of the Roman Catholic section of Walkley Cemetery, reads thus:-

PRAY FOR THE REPOSE
OF THE SOULS OF
GEORGE MOONEY,
DIED 22nd JUNE, 1961.
MARGARET,
HIS BELOVED WIFE
DIED 9th OCT. 1975
R.I.P.

CHAPTER TWELVE

AROUND AND ABOUT THE CITY

"All bright and glittering in the smokeless air."
William Wordsworth
1770-1850

SHEFFIELD, at first sight, is a city almost devoid of monuments and memorials, but with a little effort and a lot of searching it is possible to unearth a rich hoard of plaques and other small memorials. The ones that I have included in this folio are in no particular order, they are from all over the city and they all deserve a mention.

There are two plaques beside the entrance to the AEU building which stands on the roundabout which links the Arundel Gate dual carriageway with Furnival Gate. Both are in memory of leading trade unionists who left their mark on Sheffield.

The top plaque is square and the inscription is:-

JACK THOMAS MURPHY
(1888-1966)
THIS PLAQUE WAS ERECTED BY SHEFFIELD
CITY COUNCIL AND THE AMALGAMATED
ENGINEERING UNION TO COMMEMORATE THE
CENTENARY OF THE BIRTH
ON 9th DECEMBER 1888, OF JACK MURPHY,
WHO WAS A FOUNDER MEMBER OF THE
SHEFFIELD WORKERS COMMITTEE -
THE FORERUNNER OF THE ENGINEERING
SHOP STEWARDS MOVEMENT.
A PROLIFIC WRITER AND CAMPAIGNER, HIS
WORK REFLECTED THE SLOGAN OF THE
TIMES...
"EDUCATE, AGITATE, PROPOGATE."

The plaque below is an oval brass one and the inscription reads:-

GEORGE CABORN 1916-1982

GEORGE CABORN WORKED THROUGHOUT HIS LIFE FOR SOCIAL PROGRESS, AGAINST RACISM AND FOR PEACE AND FRIENDSHIP BETWEEN PEOPLES OF THE WORLD.

HE WAS AN ENGINEERING WORKER WHOSE EXPERIENCES IN THE 1930's AND THE SECOND WORLD WAR OPENED HIS EYES TO MANY INJUSTICES. HE WAS FIRST ACTIVE IN HIS UNION AS A SHOP STEWARD, THEN AS A CONVENER AT FIRTH BROWN, BECOMING DISTRICT SECRETARY OF THE AUEW FROM 1968 TO 1981. HE PLAYED A LEADING ROLE IN THE FORMATION OF THE SHEFFIELD CAMPAIGN AGAINST RACISM, CHAIRING MEETINGS FROM 1977 TO 1982. AMONG OTHER INTERESTS,

HE WAS A MEMBER OF SHEFFIELD CITY POLYTECHNIC BOARD OF GOVERNORS.

In 1981, George Caborn was awarded
the Freedom of the City of Sheffield.

George Caborn's son, Richard, is now a prominent Labour politician

These memorials give
a fair resumé
of both mens
activities.

A large metal bell used to stand, until development work, to one side of the new town hall extension. The inscription explains everything.

THE BOCHUM BELL
PRESENTED BY THE PEOPLE OF
BOCHUM TO THE PEOPLE OF
SHEFFIELD ON THE OCCASION
OF THE 35th ANNIVERSARY OF
THE TWINNING BETWEEN THEIR
CITIES
28th MAY 1986

Outside the main entrance to the city library in Surrey Street, to the right of the steps, there is an oval brass plaque which is inscribed:-

THE CITY OF SHEFFIELD
CENTRAL LIBRARY/GRAVES GALLERY
ALDERMAN JOHN GEORGE GRAVES (1866-1945)
WAS BORN IN LINCOLNSHIRE,
MOVING TO SHEFFIELD AND ESTABLISHING
SEVERAL MANUFACTURING BUSINESSES, AND
A HIGHLY SUCCESSFUL MAIL ORDER
OPERATION. A DEDICATED SALVATIONIST, HE
BECAME ONE OF THE CITY'S GREATEST
PHILANTHROPISTS, TO WHICH THE GRAVES
ART GALLERY, GRAVES PARK,
AND MUCH ELSE BESIDES TESTIFY.
THIS PLAQUE HAS BEEN SPONSORED BY
STONES BITTER

The following two items commemorate the same event

Just inside the library entrance, on the wall to the right, there is a square, stainless steel plaque. The inscription reads:-

CENTRAL LIBRARY
AND
GRAVES ART GALLERY
ERECTED WITH THE HELP OF A GIFT
BY J.G. GRAVES
DESIGNED BY W.G.DAVIES CITY ARCHITECT
OPENED IN 1934 BY HER ROYAL HIGHNESS
THE DUCHESS OF YORK
LATER QUEEN ELIZABETH

The square, bronze metal plaque on the right hand wall at the top of the entrance steps is inscribed:-

THIS BUILDING WAS OPENED BY
HER ROYAL HIGHNESS
THE DUCHESS OF YORK
ON THE FIFTH DAY OF JULY, 1934.

On the corner of the main library building, facing the city centre, there is a large oblong stone plaque. It refers to the nearby area now known as Tudor Square.This was previously covered by buildings which were demolished and the site then did duty for some time as a carpark. It bears the following inscription:-

TUDOR SQUARE
OPENED BY THE RIGHT WORSHIPFUL, THE LORD MAYOR OF SHEFFIELD
COUNCILLOR DORIS ASKHAM
ON THE 7th JUNE 1991.
THE ARTWORKS HAVE BEEN CREATED BY PAUL MASON AND FUNDED BY THE J.G.GRAVES CHARITABLE TRUST.
THE STONE WALL, MOSAICS, RAILINGS AND TREE GRILLES CELEBRATE EARLY SIGNS AND SYMBOLS OF COMMUNICATION AMONGST PEOPLE.
FROM SUCH MARKS ALL CULTURES DEVELOPED DIFFERENT ALPHABETS AND LANGUAGES.

On the corner of Castle Street and Waingate is a building, now empty, which has had a variety of names and uses over a long period of years. It was last used to house the Crown Court, which has now been removed to a new courts complex nearby. The plaque on the wall beside the main entrance explains the many other uses to which it has been put:-

COURT HOUSE 1808

ERECTED BY THE TOWN TRUSTEES AS A TOWN HALL TO DESIGNS BY WATSON OF WAKEFIELD. HAS HOUSED LOCAL GOVERNMENT, POLICE, MAGISTRATES, QUARTER SESSIONS, ASSIZES AND CROWN COURT.

Even today, over fifty years after the event, the use of an atomic bomb on the city of Hiroshima, on the mainland of Japan, is a very contentious subject. This memorial, which until the area was redeveloped, was in a quiet corner of the Peace Gardens beside the town hall, bears the following legend:-

THE HIROSHIMA MEMORIAL STONE

THE PEACE GARDENS

PREVIOUSLY NAMED ST PAUL'S GARDENS BUT CALLED BY THE PEOPLE OF SHEFFIELD, THE PEACE GARDENS, AND AS SUCH REDEDICATED ON HIROSHIMA DAY, 8th AUGUST 1985 IN THE PRESENCE OF THREE HIBAKUSHA, SURVIVORS OF THE ATOMIC DEVASTATION OF THE CITY OF HIROSHIMA. "BLESSED ARE THE PEACEMAKERS FOR THEY SHALL BE CALLED THE CHILDREN OF GOD."

CHAPTER THIRTEEN

AN HISTORIAN'S HISTORY

"The people.... unfortunately they make more history
than they can consume locally."
Hugh Hector Munro (Saki)
1870-1916

JOSEPH HUNTER

PROBABLY the writer connected to Sheffield who has the most enduring reputation is Joseph Hunter, the historian, and although many people will have heard of him, few, I suspect, will have actually read any of his work. His most famous book, "The History of Hallamshire", usually referred to simply as "Hallamshire", was first published in 1813, while his second important publication, "A History of the Deanery of Doncaster", appeared 12 years later. These books, especially "Hallamshire", are still consulted by historians today, so well researched were they and providing such an accurate picture of life in Sheffield and South Yorkshire, then known as the West Riding, at the time.

Hunter was born in 1783, but not into an academic family. His father, Michael, is described as a manufacturer, probably of cutlery and although Hunter did receive some classical education, he was apprenticed at the age of 14 years to the cutlery trade for a period of seven years. His master was William Hatfield, a maker of knives.

He served his full time and on September 24th, 1804, was admitted to the Freedom of the Cutlers' Company as a fully qualified and time served cutler. His indenture and freedom documents are now framed and hanging in the boardroom of the Cutlers Hall.

Having "served his time" and become a fully fledged cutler, Hunter immediately turned his back on his trade, despite his many years of low paid apprentice work, and entered the Unitarian College in York with the intention of becoming a minister of that church. His family were staunch members of Sheffield's Upper Chapel.

On passing out of the college, Hunter was appointed pastor of the Unitarian Church in Bath, where he leavened his religious work with his lifelong interest in historical research. His in-depth and painstaking study of old historical records marked him out as an expert on the subject and, in 1833, he began work at the Public Records Office. This must have suited him perfectly as he spent the remaining 28 years of his life there, editing and researching historical, literary and genealogical papers and records.

Outside his work at the Records Office, he enjoyed a busy life, becoming a member of the Society of Antiquaries and eventually its vice president, contributing to various literary magazines and writing articles of literary criticism.

Little is known of Hunter's marriage, except that one of his sons, Dr. Julian Hunter of Bath, presented his father's apprentice papers to the Cutlers Company and on his own death, remembered Sheffield University in his will.

When he died on May 9th, 1861, Joseph Hunter was brought home to Sheffield at his own request and was buried in Ecclesfield Churchyard at the place that he had chosen himself near to where many of his ancestors were interred. The grave can be seen today in its position about fifty yards north east of the main church building.

Hunter's family remained in the cutlery business and were a well respected company until they were taken over sometime around 1911 by Needham, Veall & Tyzack. During the firm's existence, three members of the Hunter family, in succeeding generations, had the honour of serving as Master Cutler. They were all called Michael and were elected to office in 1852, 1860 and 1903. The company, which traded as Michael Hunter & Son, had three trade marks - the bugle, granted in 1760; the bison with the Spanish word 'fuerte', meaning strong, added and the llama.

From a personal point of view, I was disappointed to see that Hunter's grave is in a very poor state of repair and has about it an air of neglect. I was very surprised to find this situation, especially as there is an apparently active Hunter Archaeological Society in the city. I would have thought that the least this society could do was to ensure that the grave of the man from whom they take their name, and who is obviously a person of some importance to the members, was a credit to them and was looked on as a place of pleasant pilgrimage which could be enjoyed by all.

At one time, the tomb appears to have had iron railings round it, but these have been cut down, possibly as a wartime salvage measure. The flat top of the tomb has a bronze relief medallion set into its surface and this depicts the Hunter family crest (pictured). The Latin inscription on the top of the tomb tells little apart from the fact that Hunter died in London on May 9th, 1861.

CHAPTER FOURTEEN

THE MUSICAL MAUSOLEUM

"I don't like 'Ebrews. They work harder; they're more sober;
They're honest and they're everywhere."
John Galsworthy
1867 - 1933

THIS is a chapter about a Jew who wasn't and a musical mausoleum which was.

Horatio Bright was the grandson of a Jewish immigrant, Isaac Bright. His father, Selim Bright, married the descendant of a Moorish princess, Estella de Lara. Horatio himself, who was born in 1828, became a successful business man and eccentric.

Following the family tradition of fruitful business dealings - his father was a prosperous watchmaker and jeweller - Horatio began work as a salesman for the cutlery firm of Turton Brothers, who operated from the former William Greaves and Sons, Sheaf Works. His career was given a huge boost when he married, in 1849, the boss's daughter, Mary Alice Turton, whose father Thomas was Master Cutler in 1846 and Mayor in 1850.

He became a partner in the firm which was then known as Turton, Bright & Co, steel manufacturers, in Cross Smithfield. Here he prospered.

His house in Crosspool, Lydgate Hall, was not huge by the standards of the day, but was said to be lavishly furnished inside with portraits and many objet d'art including collections of china, silver and furniture. The grounds surrounding the house were extensive and Horatio was able to indulge in his love of horses. It was his habit to always have five ready for the road, four for his carriage and one for the outrider. He was that wealthy.

He bought a large house, Crawshaw Hall, at Hollow Meadows, several miles outside Stannington. Here he also purchased a sloping strip of land with the intention of using it, in the future, for the burial of his close family.

He had renounced his Jewish faith some years earlier, but this didn't prevent him from contributing generously towards the building fund for the North Church Street Synagogue as well as many other good causes.

When Sam Sykes Turton Bright, his only child, married an actress, which in those days was frowned on by the gentry, Horatio never really forgave him, although he was himself to follow that course in later life when he was a widower. He doted on his grand children, especially Mary.

In 1891, Horatio's wife died and his life changed radically. She was buried in the small mausoleum that he'd built on his private cemetery and the coffin was fitted with a glass panel so that he could see her during his frequent visits. He had the small building furnished with pictures, statues and ornaments and installed a small, hand operated organ on which he played funeral music. Within three months of his wife's death, his son, Sam, followed her to the grave.

Horatio Bright's secret cemetery 1997

His business suffered from this obsession with his dead wife and he finally sold it for what was described as "a song" to William Jessop & Sons Ltd.

Although it must appear from his actions that he was eternally devoted to his dead wife and her memory, he married again aged 70 years old and this second marriage, to an actress, Minnie Harl or Hart, yielded him three children, although he was 45 years older than his wife.

When he died, in 1905, his funeral was a secret affair, his coffin being delivered to the cemetery, on a cart, beneath a load of wood. He was a rich, if confused old man, leaving an estate worth £137,000. This included the sum of £1,000 towards the upkeep of his secret cemetery and its musical mausoleum.

At the time of writing this, the site is overgrown and derelict. There are two small buildings at the top of the hill, both of which are empty, together with a heap of rubble which may be the remains of a third building and five family gravestones set into the surface of a flat-topped, raised piece of ground plus many wind bent and stunted trees. Underfoot the ground is carpeted with weeds and lank grass. Even the iron gate, which is the only way in, is creaking with rust and disuse. It is altogether a desolate and God forsaken place - but whose God?

The inscriptions on the five gravestones read:-

EMILY BELINDA BRIGHT,
BORN 23rd JULY,1834,
DIED 20th APRIL, 1885.

****

EDMUND SAMPSON
BRIGHT,
DIED MARCH 23rd, 1848,
AGED 16.

****

FREDERICK BRIGHT,
DIED JUNE 24th, 1898,
AGED 70.

****

HENRIETTA BRIGHT,
DIED AUGUST 24th, 1863,
AGED 58.

ESTELLA BRIGHT,
DIED AUG. 20th 1878.
SELIM BRIGHT,
HUSBAND OF THE
ABOVE,
DIED JAN. 8th 1891.
AUGUSTUS BRIGHT,
DIED NOV. 1st 1880.
OCTAVIOUS BRIGHT,
DIED 1892.
SONS OF THE ABOVE

CHAPTER FIFTEEN

THE GREAT SHEFFIELD FLOOD

"The waters went wild o'er his child and he was left lamenting."

Thomas Campbell

1777 - 1844

ONE wet and cold night, when gales were howling down the valley and vicious squalls of torrential rain beat out tattoos on shuttered windows, a combination of the appalling weather, poor communications, construction errors and human failings set in motion the chain of events which culminated in the tragedy which is referred to today as The Great Sheffield Flood. It happened on the night of 11th & 12th March, 1864.

It was pitch dark and very late in the evening when a man noticed that the huge earth bank which formed the dam of Dale Dyke reservoir was cracked and leaking. By then it was too late and within a matter of a couple of hours the whole structure had collapsed and millions of gallons of water burst free and became a mad deluge which swept down the Loxley Valley, through Malin Bridge and Hillsborough and down Penistone Road towards the town centre. The trail of destruction was immense.

The dam held back 114,000,000 cubic feet of water, that is a dead weight of 1,385,600 tons. In three quarters of an hour, the reservoir was empty and this huge weight of water had roared away towards Sheffield.

The total number of people who were killed, either drowned or smashed to death, was 240; about 700 animals were killed; 15 bridges and about 100 buildings of assorted types were destroyed and 4,000 houses were either damaged or flooded. It must have been an absolutely terrifying spectacle.

Rolling mills, water wheels and cutlery forges were swept away or smashed beyond repair and many people were either drowned immediately or swept away to be found later miles away. Two bodies were in fact pulled out of the River Don at Mexborough and their graves can be seen today in the local churchyard.

The following graves are in Wadsley Parish Churchyard and there are others scattered around various locations in the city. All of the inscriptions are well worth reading. The often quaint wording used in those days sometimes refers to the flood as the Bradfield Inundation.

Mr Thomas Harrison's tilt mill and forge was swept away in the flood leaving only the water wheel. Two young men lost their lives at this site. Joe Gregory was working a full night shift with William Booth, aged 16 years. The family of Joe were able to give his body a decent burial as it was found next day about half a mile from the mill at Malin Bridge. The remains of Walter Booth were included in the "unidentified" list! There were many such bodies and this gives some indication of the damage that was caused to the fleshly remains of many of the flood victims and to its awful destructive power.

IN AFFECTIONATE REMEMBERANCE OF
JOE WILLIAM BRADBURY,
SON OF ELIJAH AND ANNIS GREGORY,
WHO WAS DROWNED IN THE INUNDATION ON
SATURDAY MORNING, ABOUT ONE O'CLOCK
MARCH 12TH 1864,WHILE ENGAGED AT
Mr HARRISON'S TILT, LOXLEY BOTTOM.
AGED 20 YEARS.
READER, TAKE THOUGHT THO (sic) THOU BE
YOUNG AND GAY,SUDDEN DEATH MAY CROSS
THY YOUTHFUL WAY;LIFE'S SLENDER THREAD,
YOU SEE, WAS BROKE SO SOON;MY MORNING
SUN WAS SET BEFORE 'TWAS NOON.

Also in the grave are his parents and brother.

IN AFFECTIONATE REMEMBERANCE
OF SARAH ANN,
THE BELOVED WIFE
OF WILLIAM WATSON, AGED 32 YEARS.
ALSO OF CAROLINE OAKLEY,
DAUGHTER OF THE ABOVE,
AGED 9 YEARS AND 11 MONTHS.
ALSO OF GEORGE HENRY, SON OF THE ABOVE
AGED 4 YEARS, WHO WERE DROWNED IN THE
GREAT FLOOD AT MALIN BRIDGE

MARCH 12th 1864.
AMID THE SOLEMN MIDNIGHT HOUR,
BORNE BY THE FLOOD WITH MIGHTY POWER,
THEY SUNK BENEATH A WATERY GRAVE,
INTO HIS ARMS WHO'S STRONG TO SAVE.
ALSO ANNIE LOUISA, DAUGHTER OF
THE ABOVE WHO DIED JUNE 22nd 1863,
AGED 10 YEARS AND 10 MONTHS.

The Watson family lived in one of a row of 12 cottages and two shops which stood at Malin Bridge, on the left hand side of the River Loxley. When the flood hit, the complete row was swept away and it was said that, "no-one could have imagined the site had ever been occupied by human dwellings!"

William Watson, his wife and their two children, together with Sarah Ann's father, were washed down the course of the river by the flood. Only William managed to survive having been separated from his family and carried up against a nearby house amongst a raft of debris to which he had clung. The inmates of the house pulled his naked and exhausted body inside through a bedroom window.

Part inscription

ALSO CHARLOTTE, RELICT OF THE ABOVE,
THOMAS TAYLOR,
SHE WAS DROWNED IN THE GREAT
FLOOD AT MALIN BRIDGE
MARCH 12th 1864, AGED 42 YEARS
"IN THE MIDST OF LIFE WE ARE IN DEATH."

Also mentioned on the gravestone are her husband and six children who died either in infancy or in early childhood.

This grave is next to the previous one
Part inscription

ALSO ANNE, RELICT OF THE ABOVE,
SAMUEL MOUNT,
SHE WAS DROWNED IN THE GREAT FLOOD,
AT MALIN BRIDGE, MARCH 12th 1864,
AGED 40 YEARS.
"SUDDEN THE GUSH 'TWAS THUS SHE FELL,
NOT EVEN TIME TO BID HER FRIENDS
FAREWELL."

IN MEMORY OF
CHARLES PRICE,
AGE ABOUT 50 YEARS.
ALSO ELIZABETH, HIS WIFE
AGE ABOUT 50 YEARS.
ALSO, EDWARD, SON OF THE ABOVE
AGE ABOUT 24 YEARS.
ALSO SARAH, HIS WIFE
AGE ABOUT 24 YEARS.
ALSO JOHN CHARLES, THEIR SON
AGE 1 YEAR AND 8 MONTHS.
ALSO INFANT. 2 DAYS OLD.
ALL RESIDING AT MALIN BRIDGE:
WERE DROWNED IN THE FLOOD CAUSED
BY THE BURSTING OF THE
BRADFIELD RESERVOIR. MARCH 12th 1864.
ALSO IN MEMORY OF GEORGE PRESTON
WHO DIED JAN 16th 1865. AGED 36 YEARS.
LIKE CROWNED FOREST TREES WE STAND,
AND SOME ARE MARK'D TO FALL.
THE AXE WILL SMITE AT GOD'S COMMAND,
AND SOON SHALL SMITE US ALL.

These two graves from the churchyard of the former Loxley United Reformed Church are situated right beside the course taken by the "great flood".

IN AFFECTIONATE REMEMBERANCE OF
HANNAH ELIZABETH,
THE BELOVED DAUGHTER OF
JOHN AND HANNAH CROWNSHAW,
WHO WAS DROWNED IN THE INUNDATION, AT
MALIN BRIDGE.
MARCH 12th 1864, AGED 17 YEARS.
THE ROSE IN ITS BEAUTIFUL BLOOM,
THE SUN'S BRIGHTEST GLORIES DECLINE;
SO EARLY CAME I TO THE TOMB,
REPENT LEST THE CASE SHOULD BE THINE.
THE BUSY TRIBES OF FLESH AND BLOOD,
WITH ALL THEIR CARES AND FEARS;
ARE CARRIED ONWARD BY THE FLOOD,
AND LOST FOLLOWING YEARS.

The young girl commemorated on the stone was a servant at The Stag Inn, Malin Bridge, which is mentioned in the next account. She had only worked at the inn for a few days prior to the flood. The verse on her grave is a rather strange piece of funerary poetry.

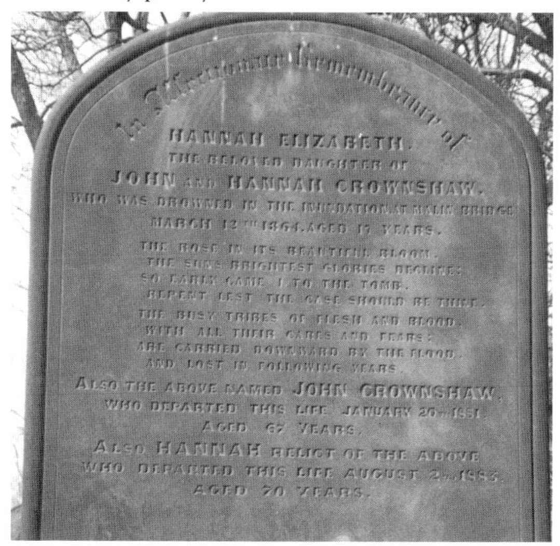

This "flood" grave mentions three young children whose bodies were never recovered. This gives some indication of the terrifying force of the wall of water which stormed down the Loxley Valley. The Stag Inn at Malin Bridge was right in the path of this flood and it was destroyed and the inhabitants, who are named on the stone below, were drowned. It would appear that William and Ann Armitage were the innkeepers of The Stag Inn. To the rear of the inn were a group of cottages. These were also destroyed with dreadful loss of life, including Greaves Armitage, brother of William, his wife and family. The body of Mrs Eliza Armitage was reported to have been found wearing nothing but a pair of stockings, her clothes having been torn off by the force of the torrent.

IN AFFECTIONATE REMEMBERANCE OF
ELIZA ARMITAGE,
AGED 67 YEARS.
ALSO HER TWO SONS AND THEIR WIVES,
AND SEVEN CHILDREN, WHO WERE ALL
DROWNED AT MALIN BRIDGE,
BY THE BRADFIELD INUNDATION, SATURDAY
MARCH 12th 1864. SEVEN OF WHOM WERE
INTERRED HERE
MARCH 16th

THOSE MARKED THUS *(HAVE NOT BEEN FOUND)

WILLIAM ARMITAGE
AGED 36 YEARS.
ALSO HIS WIFE ANN,
AGED 42 YEARS
AND THEIR 5 CHILDREN
CHARLES, aged 11 YEARS.
HENRY, aged 9 YEARS.
SAMUEL, aged 7 YEARS.
WILLIAM, aged 4 YEARS.
AND * MARIA, aged 2 YEARS.

GREAVES ARMITAGE
AGED 28 YEARS.
ALSO HIS WIFE MARIA,
AGED 30 YEARS.
AND THEIR 2 CHILDREN
*MARY, aged 3 YEARS.
*ELIZABETH, aged 4 Mths

THE EVILS THAT BESET OUR PATH,
WHO CAN PREVENT AND CURE;
WE STAND UPON THE BRINK OF DEATH,
WHEN MOST WE SEEM SECURE;
IF WE TODAY SWEET PEACE POSSESS,
IT SOON MAY BE WITHDRAWN;
SOME CHANGE MAY PLUNGE US IN DISTRESS,
BEFORE TOMORROWS DAWN.

This lone grave of a flood victim has been toppled over and lies flat on the ground in the churchyard of St John the Baptist, Chapeltown. It commemorates a young women who was a long walk from her home when she was drowned. Unless she had a horse, walking would have been the only way that she could have travelled in 1864.

IN
MEMORY OF
HANNAH MARIA,
DAUGHTER OF JACOB AND
ELIZABETH HILL,
OF MORTOMLEY, WHO WAS DROWNED
IN THE BRADFIELD INUNDATION
MARCH 12th 1864, AGED 19 YEARS.
YE KNOW NOT WHAT SHALL BE ON THE
MORROW.

CHAPTER SIXTEEN

THE FOUR LINE FLATTERY

"The cup is bitter, the sting severe,
To part with him we loved so dear;
His loss is great - we'll not complain,
But hope to meet in heaven again."

From a grave in Burngreave Cemetery.

MANY gravestones, especially those dating from the 19th century and earlier, carry brief, usually but not always, four line poems in praise of the incumbent of the grave; or pointing out to anyone bored enough to stop and read it, how miserable a place the world is to live in and how much better off the deceased are now that they have died. Sometimes, the poem is written in the first person as though the late individual had penned it themselves. Perhaps they did, given the well known pre-occupation with death and the hereafter that obsessed many Victorians.

They are a privilege to read and good fun, especially from this side of the grave and the person they describe won't surely be bothered by what is written on their gravestones. I have often wondered whether the various, and in those days, numerous stone masons had a book with them all listed down - " Number 18A is always popular, Madam"! I have seen too many which are almost the same to think that each set of lines was composed by the sobbing relatives as they sat round the coffin in a darkened room.

Just once or twice, it would be a refreshing change and would help to strip away many layers of hypocrisy if the truth about the person in the grave was actually chiselled into the stone. We are all mixtures of good, bad, stupid, selfish and lazy. None of us are pure as the driven snow, thank God. Not me, anyway!

This little verse which follows is taken from a gravestone in Wardsend Cemetery. The boy it describes was only 12 years old when he died in 1875.

AFFLICTED AS THOU WAS, DEAR CHILD,
THOU BORE IT WITH CONTENT;
WITH HUMBLE PATIENCE EVER MILD,
THOU LEFT US TO LAMENT.

This is all very nice, but in my experience, there can be very few 12 year old boys who suffer anything "with humble patience".

This grave can also be found in Wardsend Cemetery. It contains the remains of Joel Roebuck, who died in 1871 and it is written with a certain amount of grim flair.

WE LAY YOU IN YOUR NARROW BED,
AND PAY AFFECTIONS LATEST DEBT,
AS ON YOUR DARK COLD GRAVE WE SHED,
THE TEARS OF FOND AND SAD REGRET.

In the churchyard which surrounds Handsworth Church there are two graves which bear the same verse. One is to a three year old girl, who died in 1858 and the other is from a slightly older grave of 1842, which commemorates a two year old boy. Both headstones are in fine condition and attractive to look at.

THIS LOVELY BUD SO YOUNG AND FAIR,
CALL'D HENCE BY EARLY DOOM;
JUST CAME TO SHOW HOW SWEET A FLOWER,
IN PARADISE WOULD BLOOM.

Also in Handsworth churchyard, this grave carries the popular dire warning to passers-by which were often carved upon graves of this period, 1851.

MORTALS, BE READY FOR YOUR CALL,
THINK HOW SUDDEN WAS MY FALL;
GOD DOES NOT ALWAYS WARNING GIVE,
OR I MIGHT HAVE LONGER LIVED.

This offering from Handsworth churchyard is absolutely brilliant and original.

LIKE NIMROD I DID RANGE THE FIELD
FOR GAME WITH DOG AND GUN:
TILL GOD DID PLEASE TO MAKE ME YIELD
IN FATAL RIVER DUN.
A WARNING TAKE MY COMRADES ALL
OF DRINKING TO EXCESS;
BE READY WHEN THE LORD DOTH CALL
THAT HE MAY YE ALL BLESS.

They don't write them like that anymore. The River Dun is the old name for the River Don.

Darnall Cemetery has a rich crop of funerary verse and these seem to usually date from the late 19th Century until very early in the 20th century. The following one is a truncated two lines only, but the message is straight to the point.

GO HOME DEAR WIFE AND DRY YOUR TEARS,
I MUST LIE HERE TILL CHRIST APPEARS.

Not far away, in the same cemetery, is one written in the first person.

WHEN THE SOFT DEWS OF KINDLY SLEEP,
MY WEARIED EYELIDS GENTLY STEEP,
BE MY LAST THOUGHT HOW SWEET TO REST,
FOR EVER ON MY SAVIOUR's BREAST.

Also in Darnall Cemtery and written in the first person, is this verse which is a popular one. Only the first line is usually changed to suit the circumstances.

FAREWELL MY FRIENDS AND CHILDREN
DEAR, YOU LOVED ME FAITHFULLY WHILE
I WAS HERE; GRIEVE NOT FOR ME NOR
SORROW MAKE, BUT LOVE EACH OTHER
FOR MY SAKE.

This final poetic effort is again from Handsworth churchyard and is taken from a very old gravestone dated about 1800. The engraving is in poor condition and it took a fair amount of work with a brush and scraper to make sense of the following lines of priceless poetry. The final word at the end of line four I don't understand. It appears to be "coin". Whether this is an old Yorkshire dialect word I don't know. I do know that it doesn't rhyme.

REMEMBER YOU THAT VIEW THIS STONE,
YOU HAVE NO TIME TO CALL YOUR OWN,
THE LORD WILL TO HIS TEMPLE COME,
PREPARE YOUR HEART AND HE WILL MAKE
YOUR COIN.

It is still a nicely threatening little piece of doggerel with which to decorate a gravestone. I find it distressing to be constantly remined that life is so short!

I was going to end this book with the poem above, but I recently discovered this little gem while I was wandering around Attercliffe Cemetery. It is worthy of its position as the "final word"! It comes from the grave of Alfred Hobson, who died aged 23 in 1869. He is buried together with his infant son:-

SEIZE - MORTALS - SEIZE THE TRANSIENT HOURS:
IMPROVE EACH MOMENT AS IT FLIES.
LIFE'S A SHORT SUMMER: MAN'S A FLOWER:
HE DIES - ALAS: HOW SOON HE DIES.

After that, there isn't much left to say, is there?

THE END

Watch out for this bloke – he will be back!

You have just read, and I hope enjoyed, the first volume,
or folio - call it what you will - of my delvings into the
secrets of Sheffield.
Many famous names are missing from this book, but rest assured
that they will be in one of the following collections.
If they are worthwhile and interesting, they will be included.
Plus, no doubt, many photographs and little write-ups
about ordinary people.
I hope to entertain and interest you again soon!

Prints of the photographs which appear
in this book may be obtained from
Stephen J. Reaney on (0114) 246 3919

PAX VOBISCUM